Lecture Notes in Computer Science 7396

Commenced Publication in 1973
Founding and Former Series Editors:
Gerhard Goos, Juris Hartmanis, and Jan van Leeuwen

Jyrki Huusko   Hermann de Meer
Sonja Klingert   Andrey Somov (Eds.)

Energy Efficient Data Centers

First International Workshop, E^{2}DC 2012
Madrid, Spain, May 8, 2012
Revised Selected Papers

 Springer

Volume Editors

Jyrki Huusko
VTT Technical Research Centre, ICT/Network Technologies
90571 Oulu, Finland
E-mail: jyrki.huusko@vtt.fi

Hermann de Meer
University of Passau, Faculty of Computer Science & Mathematics
94032 Passau, Germany
E-mail: hermann.demeer@uni-passau.de

Sonja Klingert
University of Mannheim, Software Engineering Group
Mannheim, Germany
E-mail: klingert@informatik.uni-mannheim.de

Andrey Somov
CREAT-NET, Trento, TN 38123, Italy
E-mail: asomov@create-net.org

ISSN 0302-9743   e-ISSN 1611-3349
ISBN 978-3-642-33644-7   e-ISBN 978-3-642-33645-4
DOI 10.1007/978-3-642-33645-4
Springer Heidelberg Dordrecht London New York

Library of Congress Control Number: 2012947418

CR Subject Classification (1998): H.2.4, H.2.7-8, C.4, C.2.0-1, C.2.3-4, J.2, J.7,
K.4.3, K.6.2, I.6.6-7, B.4.2, G.1.6, F.2.2, B.8

LNCS Sublibrary: SL 5
Computer Communication Networks and Telecommunications

Typesetting: Camera-ready by author, data conversion by Scientific Publishing Services, Chennai, India

Printed on acid-free paper

Springer is part of Springer Science+Business Media (www.springer.com)

Preface

In the last decade, energy awareness has been slowly but continuously dominating our thoughts in business and private life. In the first phase, we might have only naively switched off lights when not needed or turned off our desktop during the nights, but nowadays we are prioritizing in a more sophisticated way how we can dynamically achieve the biggest impact. One of the areas that has proven to make a difference is ICT, not only through the effect that, owing to its pervasiveness, it has on other sectors; but also because of the substantial amount of 830 $MtCO_2$ [1] that the ICT sector itself (2007) is devouring world-wide.

Within ICT, with a share of 14% [1] at the global ICT carbon footprint (2007), data centers, while still not accounting for the lion share of consumption, are nevertheless the fastest growing sector that is estimated to increase its share by more than 25% until 2020. That observation was reason enough for us to launch the First International Workshop on Energy-Efficient Data Centers, E^2DC 2012, in order to increase the international recognition of energy-aware data center technologies, fostering lively exchange of ideas and interaction among participants. It was collocated with the e-Energy conference and took place in Madrid, Spain, on May 8, 2012, and was organized by the EU FP7 FIT4Green project.

The workshop resulted in these proceedings, with a scope ranging from information and communication technologies of green data centers to business models and GreenSLA solutions. The first section presents contributions in the form of position and short papers, related to various European projects. The other two sections comprise papers with more in-depth technical details. The topics covered include energy-efficient data center management and service delivery as well as energy monitoring and optimization techniques for data centers.

The first part of the proceedings contains five papers introducing research in the context of European projects and initiatives. The papers include, for example, an overview about research relating to green service level agreement extensions to establish and improve collaboration between different actors in the data center energy provisioning ecosystem (All4Green) as well as an introduction to green performance indicator definitions and benchmarking tools for data center software and hardware (GAMES). Related to service level agreements, a new standards-based solution is introduced to dynamically create service level agreements between cloud service providers/end-users and infrastructure providers (OPTIMIS). In addition, a new advanced simulation and visualization toolkit is presented for modeling and analyzing the data center energy

---

[1] Webb, M. et al.: SMART 2020: Enabling the low carbon economy in the information age. The Climate Group London.
DOI: http://www.ecoc2008.org/documents/SYMPTu_Webb.pdf, 2008

efficiency (CoolEmAll). The final paper of the first part presents an implementation of benchmarking tools, which can show explicitly the energy- and cost-saving potential in data centers.

Part 2 presents four papers on energy-efficient data center management and service delivery. The topics of the papers vary from cloud computing and virtualization systems to dynamic service level agreement based, or SLA-based, server hardware management and GreenSLA management. For example, Drazen Lucanin et al. consider an emission trading market and decision model for a greenhouse gas trading system for data centers, whereas the paper of Vlasia Anagnostopoulou concentrates on the SLA-based resource management for resource-demanding Internet services. Marco Guazzone et al. introduce a virtual machine migration-based concept for system-level energy consumption minimization for infrastructure-as-a-service (IAAS) cloud systems. In their contribution on data center management, Christian Bunse et al. suggest utilizing GreenSLAs for the energy optimization and system control from a service provider point of view.

Part 3 on "Data Center Energy Monitoring and Optimization" provides insight into more focused solutions to monitor and measure data center services. One main aspect is the data center federation, in which data center services are distributed in geographically different locations, also utilizing various energy and cooling sources with different emission characteristics. Mikko Pervilä et al. present in their paper a low-cost and quick way to model a data center's air flow and temperature characteristics, without extensive and resource-demanding simulations. Edward Curry et al. suggest an environmental charge-back model, which can be used for indicating the data center's environmental impact directly to consumers. The contribution by Dang Ming Quan et al. addresses energy optimizing opportunities of a data center federation and proposes a new resource optimization algorithm to minimize the power consumption and carbon dioxide emissions in a federated data center scenario. Using a bionic approach, Ghislain Chetsa et al. present a DNA-inspired energy consumption optimization model for high-performance computing systems.

In total, 32 papers related to energy efficiency aspects of data centers were submitted, 13 of which were selected through a peer-reviewed process for publication in these proceedings. The workshop also included three additional presentations: The FIT4Green project approach by Giovanni Giuliani (HP Italy Innovation Centre, Italy), the keynote speech by Marta Chinnici (ENEA, Italian National Agency for New Technology, Italy), and a presentation about a new energy-efficient data center facility initiative, which targets to re-utilize the unused paper mill facilities in Nordic countries, by Kimmo Koski.

We would like to thank all authors for their contributions to this volume and in particular the reviewers for their hard work which significantly helped to improve the initial submissions and made our work easier when selecting the papers. We would like to also thank all volunteers who shared their talent, dedication, and time for the workshop arrangements and for preparing these proceedings: Special thanks are extended to the e-Energy 2012 Organizing Committee and especially to Antonio Fernandez Anta and Rebeca de Miguel (Institute IMDEA Networks, Spain), for their continuing support and generously provided help in organizing the workshop co-located with e-Energy 2012. We would also like to thank Springer LNCS for organizational support in preparing the proceedings and Sherwette Abdeen (University of Mannheim, Germany) for arranging the manuscripts.

Last but not least, we are grateful for the strong support from the European Commission and the ICT FP7 FIT4Green project, especially from Maria Pérez Ortega (GFI, Spain) and Giovanni Giuliani (HP Italy Innovation Centre, Italy).

May 2012   Jyrki Huusko
                                                              Hermann de Meer
                                                               Sonja Klingert
                                                               Andrey Somov

Organization

Workshop Chairs

Jyrki Huusko   VTT Technical Research Centre of Finland,
                            Finland
Hermann de Meer   University of Passau, Germany

Publication Chairs

Sonja Klingert   University of Mannheim, Germany
Andrey Somov   CREATE-NET, Italy

Technical Program Committee

Colin Atkinson   University of Mannheim, Germany
Robert Basmadjian   University of Passau, Germany
Ivona Brandic   Vienna University of Technology, Austria
Christian Bunse   University of Applied Sciences and Stralsund,
                            Germany
George Da Costa   Université Paul Sabatier, Toulouse, France
Erol Gelenbe   Imperial College London, UK
Giovanni Giuliani   HP Italy Innovation Centre, Italy
Xavier Hesselbach-Serra   Universitat Politecnica de Catalunya, Spain
Jussi Kangasharju   University of Helsinki, Finland
Bastian Koller   High Performance Computing Centre
                            Stuttgart, Germany
Barbara Pernici   Politecnico di Milano, Italy
Tuan Anh Trinh   Budapest University of Technology and
                            Economics, Hungary
Athanasios V. Vasilakos   National Technical University of Athens,
                            Greece
Gregor von Laszewski   Indiana University, USA

Sponsoring Institutions

VTT Technical Research Centre of Finland, Finland
University of Passau, Germany
University of Mannheim, Germany
CREATE-NET, Italy
e-Energy 2012

Table of Contents

Data Center Energy Monitoring and Optimization

Setting Energy Efficiency Goals in Data Centers: The GAMES Approach

Barbara Pernici[1], Cinzia Cappiello[1], Maria Grazia Fugini[1], Pierluigi Plebani[1],
Monica Vitali[1], Ioan Salomie[2], Tudor Cioara[2], Ionut Anghel[2], Ealan Henis[3],
Ronen Kat[3], Doron Chen[3], George Goldberg[3], Micha vor dem Berge[4],
Wolfgang Christmann[4], Alexander Kipp[5], Tao Jiang[5], Jia Liu[5],
Massimo Bertoncini[6], Diego Arnone[6], and Alessandro Rossi[6]

[1] Politecnico di Milano, Italy
{pernici,cappiell,fugini,plebani,vitali}@elet.polimi.it
[2] Technical University of Cluj-Napoca, Romania
{ioan.salomie,tudor.cioara,ionut.anghel}@cs.utcluj.ro
[3] IBM Israel Science and Technology Limited, Israel
{ealan,ronenkat,cdoron,georgeg}@il.ibm.com
[4] Christmann Informationstechnik, Germany
{micha.vordemberge,wolfgang.christmann}@christmann.info
[5] University of Stuttgart, HLRS, Germany
{kipp,jiang,liu}@hlrs.de
[6] Engineering Ingegneria Informatica, Italy
{massimo.bertoncini,diego.arnone,alessandro.rossi}@eng.it

Abstract. Energy-aware service centers take into account energy consumption of infrastructures, machines, applications, storage systems, and their distributed computing architecture. The approach to energy efficiency in data centers in the GAMES (Green Active Management of Energy in IT Service centers) project is presented: Green Performance Indicators (GPIs), i.e., properties that, continuously monitored, evidence the level of consumed energy by the center's IT resources, can be the basis of a systematic approach to increase energy efficiency. The GPIs are the basis for improving energy efficiency with adaptive actions and to achieve a higher level of green maturity, as prescribed, for instance, in the GreenGrid Data Center Maturity Model (DCMM), based on a usage-centric perspective in GPIs. The paper briefly describes monitoring of GPIs and the adaptation actions adopted to reach the green goals. Preliminary experimental results are discussed.

Keywords: data centers, energy-efficiency, adaptivity, Green Performance Indicators, monitoring, control.

1 Introduction

Service centers aware of the energy they consume in terms of resources both at the software and hardware level are gaining more and more attention with the promise of developing systems that can be tuned to consume less energy

J. Huusko et al. (Eds.): E^{2}DC 2012, LNCS 7396, pp. 1–12, 2012.

for IT resources, cooling, consumables, and lower CO_2 emissions. Researches focusing on metrics and measurements for green IT and service centers are in progress with the vision of achieving economical, environmental, and technological sustainability [1,2]. To this aim, several sets of metrics have been proposed to measure service centers efficiency, e.g., as proposed by Green Grid, Uptime Institute, Transaction Performance processing Council (TPC), to mention a few. Several techniques for an efficient resource allocation and utilization in data centers based on adaptivity have been proposed, using for instance CPU frequency as an important parameter to improve energy [3][4] or proposing an efficient usage of the storage devices [5].

To sustain this attention, GAMES is centered on designing, developing, and executing applications along the perspectives of energy awareness [6], namely of services characterized by indicators regarding which IT resources, as well as what effort (e.g., in terms of costs) are required during development, execution, and maintenance [7].

The goal of this paper is to illustrate how *Green Performance Indicators* (GPIs) can be used as a comprehensive approach to monitor service centers on energy-efficiency related parameters. The GPIs are mainly based on a usage-centric perspective, to enable the assessment of the level of use of all resources in the service centers, also in relation to the services being provided by the center and their requirements and characteristics. The GAMES approach provides a systematic and scalable approach to GPI definition, monitoring, and management. On the basis of GPIs, several control actions can be performed in order to guarantee a high level of usage of resources. Given an application and its IT resources configuration (virtualized or real), a good level of utilization of resources can be achieved through monitoring and adaptation of the system configuration to avoid waste of resources. In the paper, we discuss the GAMES achievements with respect to some of the goals set by The GreenGrid[1] [8], which defines green maturity levels for data centers.

In the following of the paper, Section 2 illustrates the main GPIs considered in this paper and their relation to the GreenGrid Maturity Model goals. Section 3 describes the monitoring infrastructure to collect and memorize sensor and system data and to analyze them. In Section 4, the controllers that, based on GPIs, select adaptivity actions for improving energy efficiency are illustrated. Section 5 presents the experimental settings and, finally, Section 6 discusses how monitoring data can be used to improve the system configurations.

2   Green Performance Indicators

Starting from the whole set of GAMES GPIs (which include technical, as well as organizational, environmental, and development-related indicators), in this paper we consider only the *IT-related* and the *QoS-related* GPIs, which have

---

[1] http://www.thegreengrid.org/

Table 1. Games Contribution to GreenGrid Maturity Model

Parameter	Best Practice	Level 5	GPIs	Adapt. Actions
Compute: Utilization	CPU 20%	CPU 60%	CPU Usage	Resource Allocation
Compute: Workload	Rationalize Workload (virtualization/consolidation)	Shift all of the workload across many data centers taking into account business priorities, external drivers, availability of resource and TCO - "Follow the Moon" strategy	CPU Usage, Memory Usage, Application performance, IOPS, Energy	Resource Allocation, reconfiguration
Compute: Operations	Understand performance through the use of standard benchmarks	Improve application use of processor, memory and major power consumption components	Storage Usage	Resource Allocation
Compute: Power Management	Power Monitoring	Optimization of power with no impact over Performance	Application Performance, Energy	CPU frequency scaling, Power mgmt at server level
Storage: Operation	Storage Consolidation	Operational media choice based on TCO model. energy usage, embedded carbon footprint and business need	Storage Usage, Energy	Storage Migration
Storage: Technology	Low Power Consuming Technology	Use/enablement of low power states for storage	Storage Usage, IOPS, Energy	Acoustic disk modes

been used in the experimental setting[2]. The interested reader is referred to [9] for a complete overview on the GAMES GPIs.

In Table 1, a subset of parameters of the GreenGrid maturity model (related to IT factors) is mapped to GAMES general GPIs and a general reference to GAMES adaptation actions is given.

For instance, considering the Compute Utilization parameter, the GreenGrid Maturity Model indicates CPU usage as a parameter, set at level 20% for Level 2 (best practices) and should reach the target goal of a value greater than 60% (Level 5) by 2015. A similar approach is taken considering other parameters of the maturity model, defining appropriate GPIs, illustrated in general terms in Table 1, and refined in Table 2.

In the first column of Table 2, the main indicators used in GAMES experimentation are reported, while in the second column details of measured values are given. All indicators can be evaluated at different abstraction levels: from system level, to a cluster of servers, to application level. *CPU Usage* relates to the processor utilization percentage. *Memory Usage* refers to the usage of main memory (RAM). This indicator characterizes the percentage of occupation of RAM. *Storage Usage* denotes to which extent storage is used. This GPI denotes the storage utilization percentages for running applications in a given configuration counting files

---

[2] The terms GPI/indicator and application/service are used in an interleaved manner.

and/or device (depending on the desired granularity for the measures) accesses. Throughput and capacity usage based energy efficiency indicators are also calculated by modeling used power per device. *IOPS* characterizes the efficiency of the communication with the storage/devices accounting the number of IPOS operations that can be executed in a time unit using a single Watt for a device or for storage. *Application Performance* measures energy consumption per computed unit, e.g., number of Transactions/kWh or GFLOPS/kWh. This indicator is given in *ComputationUnit/KWh*. *Response Time (RT)* is a performance GPI, related to QoS, measuring the time taken by a service S to handle user requests (measuring the delay between the moment a service request is sent and the moment the service is rendered). It can be measured also at the infrastructure level, e.g., on storage access as disk response time.

Table 2. Main GAMES GPIs

GPI	Measured values
CPU Usage	measured directly (%)
Memory Usage	measured directly (%)
Storage Usage	disk/file access counters, throughput and capacity usage, disk-used-capacity/W
IOPS	IOPS/W, Disk IOP rate, Device IOPS, Disk-throughput/W
Application perfor-mance	Transactions/Energy, GFLOPs/KWh
Energy	measured directly
Response Time (RT)	execution time at server (ms), disk response time

3   Monitoring IT Components in Data centers

To be able to compute the GPIs, testbed has been set up focusing on a wide variety of different test options and fine-grained monitoring. The detailed architecture of the GAMES infrastructure is described in [10] and it outside the scope of this paper. In Section 3.1, we provide a general description of the monitoring infrastructure, while in Section 3.2 we describe the system to analyze and store information deriving from monitoring and to make it accessible to the controllers which enforce the adaptation actions.

3.1   Monitoring Infrastructure

For monitoring, the testbed has been set up considering the following main elements:

- Infrastructure Servers, providing all necessary services for a network;
- a gigabit Ethernet switch;
- a Boot Server, enabling to easily switch the service systems execution on the various computing nodes;

- a Storage Server, equipped with different types of hard drives;
- a Power Distribution Unit, with an integrated power meter measuring the power consumption of the storage, switch and infrastructure servers;
- a RECS (Resource Efficient Computing System) Cluster Server, with 18 integrated computing nodes and a dedicated, system-independent monitoring architecture.

The Storage Server and the RECS Cluster Server[3] are the main testbed components. The latter offers computing capabilities of 18 CPUs that can be centrally managed. To avoid influencing the results by bothering the nodes to get sensor data, a new monitoring approach has been designed and a Cluster Server has been built. The core concepts are: i) reduce network load; ii) avoid the dependency of polling each node at the operating system layer; iii) build up a basis for new monitoring and controlling concepts. These requirements have been implemented via a dedicated master-slave architecture of microprocessors that collect the most important sensor values from each single compute node, such as status (on/off), temperature of the main board and power consumption. Every node is connected to a slave micro-controller locally gathering these metrics. Then, the master micro-controller centrally collects all information. This master micro-controller is accessible to the user by a dedicated network port and has to be read out only once to get all information about the installed computing nodes. If a user monitors e.g., 10 metrics on all 18 nodes, he would have to perform 180 pulls. These can now be reduced to one, since the master does a pre-aggregation and processing of the monitoring data. This example shows the immense capabilities of a dedicated monitoring architecture.

For storage usage, file/block level statistics are collected via special purpose monitoring agents to relate them to applications.

To collect all low-level, or directly measurable, metrics, the Nagios monitoring tool is employed. Nagios allows using a wide variety of available plug-ins to gather most typical metrics from servers like memory usage or CPU usage. In addition, some own plug-ins have been developed to read out the RECS Cluster Server micro-controller and the power distribution unit with the integrated power meter. Historically grown, many of the public Nagios plug-ins have different ways of storing their information to the database. To get a common data set, to aggregate and normalize these metrics, a pre-processing is performed (see [11]).

3.2 Providing Information to Controllers

One key aspect is how information flows from the monitoring infrastructure to the controllers which enforce adaptivity actions. The *Energy Sensing and Monitoring Infrastructure* subsystem is in charge of collecting, processing and dispatching data from the service center IT infrastructure and environmental sensors. Its *Infrastructure Access Module* component captures energy, performance and context data at different layers: facilities, single server (compute

---

[3] A detailed description of the RECS is at http://shared.christmann.info/download/project-recs.pdf

node), cluster server, storage system and virtual systems (virtual machines, virtual storage and application container).

Once collected, raw monitoring data are analyzed. The *Finalised Context Interface Monitor* component parses, refines and organizes raw data into structured run-time energy/performance data (context data) for the rest of the platform. Context data collected and processed in real time refer to: IT infrastructure energy/performance data, environmental data and the state of the GAMES-enabled applications running on the service center. The GPIs are evaluated starting from context data and the results are collected and stored into the *Energy Practice Knowledge Base* which eventually contains all information about configuration and status of the service center.

Besides the main service-oriented architecture of the communication system, an event-based architecture is provided to support asynchronous notifications by means of a *Provenance Tracking Interface* module. Various classes of events are specified ranging from classes regarding the start-end of executions to actions required to adapt the system.

4 Control Actions

A set of controllers are set in place to analyze the GPIs and energy consumption on the various devices and to enable control actions able to change the state/configuration of components to save energy. The controllers are described in the following sections. Table 3 summarizes the features of the Energy Aware Self-* Controller and of the Storage Controllers.

4.1 GAMES Energy Controllers

The Energy Aware Self-* Controllers combine techniques like context- and energy-aware computing, autonomic computing and self-adapting control. Run-time energy efficiency is addressed by two types of control loops: (i) a set of Local Control Loops which take adaptation decisions at each server level and (ii) a Global Control Loop which takes adaptation decisions at the whole service center level.

The *Local Control Loops* exploit the energy saving opportunities given by short-term fluctuations in the performance request levels of the servers' running tasks. The adaptation actions at each server level are: (i) put server CPU to Sleep State (C-3) when no workload is executed and (ii) execute transitions between CPU performance states (P-states) according to the workload characteristics when the CPU is in the Operating State (C-0). When deciding to change the P-State of the CPU, the Local Control Loop computes the trade-off between performance and energy by considering that the higher the P-State, the more the power consumed by the CPU. In a lower P-State, the CPU performance degradation will increase. For the Local Control Loop, an adaptation decision methodology is defined inspired from the human immune system biological structures and processes defending a living organism against diseases [12]. The server is monitored to gather CPU-related power/performance data which is then formally represented using an antigen inspired model.

Table 3. GAMES Energy Aware Self-* Controller

Energy Aware Self-* Controller	Method	Input GPIs	Adaptation Actions
Local Loop Control (LLC)	human immune system inspired	CPU usage, Application Performance	Dynamic Frequency Scaling action
Global Loop Control (GLC)	Self-adaptation control, reasoning-based evaluation, reinforcement learning	CPU usage, Memory usage, Application performance, RT	Dynamic Power Management at server level, Workload consolidation, resource provisioning
Storage Management Controller	**Method**	**Input GPIs**	**Actions**
Disk Acoustic mode Control Loop	Fuzzy Inference System (FIS)	Disk IOP rate Sequential access ratio, Disk response time	Set disk acoustic mode (Normal/Quiet)
Storage placement Control Loop	File splitting into chunks, usage centric energy efficiency ranking of storage devices	Device IOPS, throughput and capacity usage	Split application file into chunks, Initial chunk placement based on device rank, Chunk migration based on device rank and chunk usage statistics

The *Global Control Loop* minimizes the service center energy consumption by pro-actively detecting the service center over-provisioned hardware computing resources and dynamically adapting, at run time, the allocated computing resources to the workload intensity changes. A self-adaptation function associates to each energy-inefficient state of the service center (i.e., a non-green state where the GPIs levels defined at design-time are not reached) an adaptation action plan [13]. To identify energy-inefficient states, an Energy Aware Context Model and ontology are defined to evaluate the GPIs through reasoning based techniques. The adaptation methodology is based on reinforcement learning and gives the following types of adaptation actions: (i) energy-aware resource provisioning and consolidation in the middleware (e.g. provisioning of hardware resources to virtual tasks, or virtual tasks deployment or migration) and (ii) dynamic power management actions at the hardware level (such as hibernate/wake-up servers).

4.2 Storage Controllers

The GAMES storage management system achieves storage energy efficiency by using two controllers: (i) the Disk Mode Controller, controlling the disk acoustic mode, and (ii) the Chunk Placement Controller, controlling the placement of application files split into chunks.

The *Disk Acustic Mode Controller* is based on a Fuzzy Inference System that leverages our previous work [14] and translates our understanding of disk power consumption under various load conditions into a set of fuzzy rules that attempt to save energy.

The *Chunk Placement Controller* splits an application file (which can be large, e.g., 200 GB) into smaller chunks (of 1 MB or smaller, for finer grained file placement), and performs two main operations: placement of a new chunk, and chunk migration. Both placement operations aim to place the chunk on a disk such that the energy it consumes will be minimized. Energy minimization is achieved by ranking the storage devices per their usage centric energy efficiency metrics. The adopted metrics for storage are disk used capacity per Watt, disk access IOPS per Watt, and disk throughput per Watt [15].

The inputs to the storage management system include application-level information (e.g., application annotations and application to file mapping) as well as file-level and block-level monitored storage data.

5   Tools Environment and First Evaluation of Results

Monitoring is implemented using Nagios and NDOUtils. The Energy Sensing and Monitoring Infrastructure Prototype is coded in Java, EJB v3.0. It is implemented as a SOA (Service Oriented Architecture) and uses Grizzly (HTTP Web Server) and Jersey (REST Service stack). The application server for the enterprise application is Glassfish. GPIs computation uses Octave, an open-source Matlab-like engine. The event system is based on the JMS middleware. The Global and Local Control Loops are implemented in Java. The former is based on an agent-oriented architecture using JADE. For monitoring and action enforcement, the Global Control Loop uses OpenNebula Java OCA API with wakeonlan and OpenSSH tools. To develop the Local Control Loop in-line power management techniques, the cpuinfo tool and Hyperic Sigar library are used for monitoring, while the cpufreq module is used to enforce the CPU P-state changes. The EACM ontology is described in OWL while the low-level GPIs are described in the SWRL language.

As a first evaluation, the simulation of a typical HPC application has been executed on a 18 nodes cluster with enhanced monitoring capabilities, each holding an Intel P8400 CPU (2x 2.26 GHz, 1066 MHz FSB) and 4GB DDR3 Dual Channel RAM. Details of the testbed environment are reflected in [10]. Tests to analyze improvements of energy efficiency in business applications have been performed using the TPC-C benchmark.

For energy control loops, the energy consumption of a testbed server has been measured at different load values by means of a power meter. The optimal energy consumption/performance tradeoff is achieved for a threshold of about 75% CPU and Memory usage, considering a standard deviation of $+/- 15\%$.

Considering the compliance with the Maturity Model goals related to CPU usage values, as a first achievement, we have a better performance both when addressing the problem in the energy control loops (around 75% +/- 15% in Global Control Loop control) and in VM configuration (threshold set at 80%), while the GreenGrid Maturity Model has a goal of 60% for level 5.

Energy consumption lines up to improvements of 5% in local control loops, 15% in global control loops, and 7% in software configuration adaptation.

6 Mining and Configuration Improvement

The data collected in the monitoring are further used to assess the system and its configuration. A mining system supports statistical investigation over GPIs, while software and hardware configuration improvements are considered for system evolution and redesign.

In Table 4, indicators used to drive the selection of hardware and software configurations and setting of thresholds are shown.

Table 4. GPIs for improvement of software and hardware configurations

	GPIs
Sw config (VM)	resource usage, RT
Hw config	resource usage, IOPS/W, application performance

6.1 Mining GPIs

GPIs are constantly monitored and their historical values are forwarded to the GAMES Data Mining module. All the measures taken on the GAMES testbed at a specific instant (i.e., in a defined time slot) constitute a finalized context instance stored into a stack containing historical values. This stack is the data source; however, mining the stack for time, resource and consequently energy consumption analysis, can require quite an effort, due to the high number of monitored parameters. A pre-processing step is performed and the computation of proper and significant indicators reduce the computational cost of the mining step, by aggregating more parameters. This also permits to interpret the extracted patterns, since indicators and relations among them can be easily analyzed.

Basic descriptive statistics computations are performed, such as correlation, and supervised and unsupervised data mining algorithms are applied such as association rule mining and clustering, respectively.

Correlation between two indicators A and B is a bi-variate descriptive statistics parameter that quantifies how the behavior of A affects B. This computation is performed by the Data Mining module my means of a synchronous invocation of its API. On the contrary, the APRIORI algorithm chosen for extracting *association rules* among indicators, is asynchronously invoked by a human supervisor through the Graphical User Interface of the GAMES Energy Efficiency Tool. Through the GUI, experts can perform a rule validation process by discarding spurious rules and keeping only useful and exploitable relations. Finally, *clustering* is applied to indicators related to the application layer. Discovered clusters, for instance, could split the overall space of the business processes in more subspaces each one characterized by a well defined green performance indicators related behavior, corresponding to the cluster centroid.

6.2   Software Configuration Improvement

Using Virtual Machines enables a dynamic allocation of resources to each deployed application. The design of the configuration of Virtual Machines for business transaction running the TPC-C benchmark has been analyzed. An example is shown in Table 5 where, starting from an inefficient configuration, the system continuously detects the violation of a GPI. The violated indicators are highlighted in bold. The violation of the threshold suggests the administrator to change the configuration until reaching efficiency without violating other indicators. The reconfiguration can also be automatic if rules are defined to enact a reconfiguration when a violation occurs.

Table 5. Virtual Machine reconfiguration towards energy efficiency

Step	Virtual Machine Configuration	GPI1 (App. Perf.) > 1000	GPI2 (CPU us.) > 80%	GPI3 (Storage us.) > 30%	GPI4 (IOPS/ Watt) > 100	GPI5 (Memory us.) > 75%	QoS1 (Resp. time) < 1 sec.
Step0	4 CPUs, 512 MB RAM, 10 GB HD	13822	**47.15%**	38%	133	97.96%	0.034
Step1	3 CPUs, 512 MB RAM, 10 GB HD	15080	**67.42%**	32%	175.57	93.30%	0.063
Step2	2 CPUs, 512 MB RAM, 10 GB HD	16250	99.67%	38%	107.42	97.91%	0.048

6.3   Hardware Configuration Improvement

Hardware configuration design and improvement have also been analyzed. In the experimentation on the High Performance Computing (HPC) case, the Local Control Loops tackle high energy consumption by adjusting the servers' CPU power states (P-states) according to the incoming workload variation. The HPC first trials show the Local Control Loops energy saving potential. However, the results are directly influenced by the number of P-states of the servers' CPUs. A higher number of power states will provide the Local Control Loops with more accurate control on the CPU power consumption and consequently with higher energy saving. The current HPC testbed processors Intel P8400, used for the first trials have 3 P-states (for next trials the HPC test bed servers processors will be improved to Intel i7 processors with up to 12 P-states, thus achieving better results). Another optimization for improving energy savings results is to make the Local Control Loops aware of the workload dependencies and predictability in the HPC case. In this approach, when deciding to change the processor's P-states, the Local Control Loops will take into consideration the state of the neighbor dependent processors. For example, if a server's processor enters the Idle working mode, another server processor's Local Control Loop aware of this fact (due to the workload dependency knowledge among processors) may also decide to enter the Idle mode in the near future, thus starting early the necessary preparations.

The dynamic frequency scaling decisions taken by the bio-inspired Local Control Loop are taken by learning from previous experience in a similar manner to the human immune system. The energy savings results will be improved when a workload with similar characteristics is frequently encountered in the execution history of the local loop, because the dynamic frequency scaling assignment decisions for that type of workload will have already been learned. This exactly suits the HPC case, which deals with a relatively small number of applications. A detailed analysis about the first GAMES Trial results is available at http://www.green-datacenters.eu/.

7 Concluding Remarks and Future Work

In this paper, we have presented the GAMES approach to monitoring and adapting the use of resources by service centers to save energy. We set the basis to evaluate to what extent and how the maturity model goals can be achieved in GAMES through setting *thresholds* for energy-efficiency goals, based on usage-based GPIs. Monitoring and control of indicators then suggest adaptation actions able to tune energy consumption to the needed level. By analyzing the relevant context information, the results show also that the GAMES platform can improve energy efficiency by adopting different hardware and software configurations.

Ongoing work is aimed to show the effectiveness of the designed GPIs and at evaluating the overall adaptation strategies. The initial results encourage further investigation in the direction of GPIs for energy-awareness and of monitoring and mining techniques. Further integration of modules and complete integration are being developed to enrich the monitoring infrastructure and the relevant context data analysis and mining.

Acknowledgments. This work has been partially supported by the GAMES project (http://www.green-datacenters.eu/) and has been partly funded by the European Commissions IST activity of the 7th Framework Program (contract number ICT-248514). This work expresses the opinions of the authors and not necessarily those of the European Commission. The European Commission is not liable for any use that may be made of the information contained in this work.

References

1. Nowak, A., Leymann, F., Schumm, D., Wetzstein, B.: An Architecture and Methodology for a Four-Phased Approach to Green Business Process Reengineering. In: Kranzlmüller, D., Toja, A.M. (eds.) ICT-GLOW 2011. LNCS, vol. 6868, pp. 150–164. Springer, Heidelberg (2011)
2. Berl, A., Gelenbe, E., Girolamo, M.D., Giuliani, G., de Meer, H., Quan, D.M., Pentikousis, K.: Energy-efficient cloud computing. Comput. J. 53(7), 1045–1051 (2010)

3. von Laszewski, G., Wang, L., Younge, A.J., He, X.: Power-aware scheduling of virtual machines in dvfs-enabled clusters. In: IEEE International Conference on Cluster Computing and Workshops, CLUSTER 2009, pp. 1–10 (2009)
4. Wang, Y., Wang, X., Chen, M., Zhu, X.: Power-efficient response time guarantees for virtualized enterprise servers. In: Real-Time Systems Symposium 2008, pp. 303–312 (2008)
5. Zhu, Q., Chen, Z., Tan, L., Zhou, Y., Keeton, K., Wilkes, J.: Hibernator: helping disk arrays sleep through the winter. ACM SIGOPS Operating Systems Review 39, 177–190 (2005)
6. Bertoncini, M., Pernici, B., Salomie, I., Wesner, S.: GAMES: Green Active Management of Energy in IT Service Centres. In: Soffer, P., Proper, E. (eds.) CAiSE Forum 2010. LNBIP, vol. 72, pp. 238–252. Springer, Heidelberg (2011)
7. Kipp, A., Jiang, T., Liu, J., Fugini, M.G., Vitali, M., Pernici, B., Salomie, I.: Applying green metrics to optimise the energy-consumption footprint of it service centres. International Journal of Space-Based and Situated Computing (to appear, 2012)
8. Singh, H., et al.: Data center maturity model. Technical report (2011)
9. Kipp, A., Jiang, T., Fugini, M., Salomie, I.: Layered green performance indicators. Future Generation Computer Systems 28(2), 478–489 (2012)
10. Kipp, A., Jiang, T., Liu, J., Buchholz, J., Schubert, L., vor dem Berge, M., Christmann, W.: Testbed architecture for generic, energy-aware evaluations and optimizations. In: Proc. of the First International Conference on Advanced Communications and Computation (INFOCOMP 2011), pp. 103–108 (2011)
11. Kipp, A., Liu, J., Jiang, T., Khabi, D., Kovalenko, Y., Schubert, L., vor dem Berge, M., Christmann, W.: Approach towards an energy-aware and energy-efficient high performance computing environment. In: 2011 IEEE International Conference on Intelligent Computer Communication and Processing (ICCP), pp. 493–499 (August 2011)
12. Cioara, T., Pop, C.B., Anghel, I., Salomie, I., Dinsoreanu, M., Condor, I., Mihaly, F.: Immune-inspired technique for optimizing servers energy consumption. In: Proc. of the 2010 IEEE International Conference on Intelligent Computer Communication and Processing (ICCP 2010), Cluj-Napoca, Romania, pp. 273–280 (2010)
13. Cioara, T., Anghel, I., Salomie, I., Copil, G., Moldovan, D., Pernici, B.: A context aware self-adapting algorithm for managing the energy efficiency of it service centres. Ubiquitous Computing and Communication Journal, Special Issue of 9th RoEduNet International Conference (2011)
14. Chen, D., Goldberg, G., Kahn, R., Kat, R.I., Meth, K.: Leveraging disk drive acoustic modes for power management. In: Proc. of the IEEE 26th Symposium on Mass Storage Systems and Technologies, MSST 2010, pp. 1–9 (2010)
15. Chen, D., Henis, E., Kat, R.I., Sotnikov, D., Cappiello, C., Ferreira, A.M., Pernici, B., Vitali, M., Jiang, T., Liu, J., Kipp, A.: Usage centric green performance indicators. In: Proc. of GreenMetrics 2011 (SIGMETRICS Workshop) (June 2011)

Sustainable Energy Management in Data Centers through Collaboration

Sonja Klingert[1], Andreas Berl[2], Michael Beck[3], Radu Serban[4],
Marco di Girolamo[5], Giovanni Giuliani[5], Hermann de Meer[2],
and Alfons Salden[4]

[1] University of Mannheim, Germany
klingert@informatik.uni-mannheim.de
[2] University of Passau, Germany
{berl,Hermann.deMeer}@uni-passau.de
[3] Stadtwerke Passau, Germany
michael.beck@stadtwerke-passau.de
[4] Almende BV, Rotterdam, The Netherlands
{radu,alfons}@almende.org
[5] Hewlett Packard Italiana SRL- Italy Innovation Center, Italy
{marco.digiolamo,guiliani}@hp.com

Abstract. In the current decade of rapid expansion of ubiquitous data storage and cloud computing services, the demand for data center services has seen an enormous increase which is resulting in a continuously rising pressure on the environment in terms of energy consumption and greenhouse gas (GHG) emissions. The recently started project, All4Green, explores potential ICT solutions for collaboration amongst data centers, energy providers, and end-users in order to enable energy providers to save CO2 emissions at the very source of energy conversion. This paper presents an overview of objectives and concepts of the research, discussing the so-called data centers' eco-system, the technical approach to collaboration and GreenSLAs as economic incentives.

Keywords: Green IT, Green Data center, GreenSLA, Energy Management and Energy Efficiency.

1   Introduction: The Problem

The last decade has seen a huge growth in computing. Today many companies "run on data" and the efficient and effective use of this data is an asset that ensures a company's competitiveness and agility. Together with the advent of the cloud computing paradigm this development is resulting in an increasing need for data centers. Unfortunately, data centers require a significant amount of energy (i.e., electricity), consuming about 1.5% of the world's energy supply [6], a share which is projected to even rise in future.

As the pressure on the environment originating in CO2 emissions is thus constantly increasing, the recently established research area of GreenIT is seeking

J. Huusko et al. (Eds.): E^{2}DC 2012, LNCS 7396, pp. 13–24, 2012.

for ways of reducing the energy consumption of or through ICT with data centers, due to their magnitude of energy consumption, as one major research field.

However, just saving energy in data centers alone might not be enough: it is the energy provider that creates an amount of CO_2-emissions depending on the energy sources used to generate electricity. Until now energy providers have fulfilled the energy demand of data centers elastically, organizing the energy conversion according to the needs (in terms of power) of their customers, notwithstanding the means this requires.

The same applies to the relationship between the data center and their customer: Based on performance oriented service level agreements (SLAs), the data center delivers its services as and when the end users require them without taking the environmental impact of this service delivery into account.

As long as those two relationships remain untouched, this situation of skyrocketing energy demand and its environmental impact will not change.

The newly established EU-FP7 project All4Green taps on the efficiency potential of viewing the partnership between the data center (DC), its energy provider (EP) and the data center end user (EU) as an eco-system which has the option to reduce CO_2 emissions considerably if the partners cooperate through a utility negotiation-based collaboration. For instance, during times of unanticipated high energy demand from outside the system, instead of using CO_2-intensive energy sources (such as, additional diesel generators) to accommodate this short-term demand peak, the EP can request temporary energy demand capping or decrease from the DC.

We propose a mechanism based on negotiation and rewarding end users, data centers and energy providers who are opting for more environmentally friendly Service Level Agreements (GreenSLA), and are not only taking into account the energy cost, but also the energy source and environmental cost of the services provisioned.

This paper is structured as follows: first we capture findings from related work areas (section 2), then we present an introduction to energy provision and the eco system of EP, DC and EU (section 3). We then explain strategies used to actively shape the energy demand upon the EP's request (section 4), and finally we make an attempt at estimating the impact this collaborative approach might have on the energy supply landscape.

2   Related Work

The shaping of energy consumption in DCs has recently been brought forward through green computing initiatives such as The Green Grid initiative [9], which look not only at the DC infrastructure, but also at the "useful services" in a server (at application-level).

Fit4Green [10] consolidates existing research in the area of federated DC management system engineering, extending it with respect to robust and proactive resource scheduling mechanisms for distributing system load under resource constraints and uncertainty. For these the project capitalizes on results of the research project FIT4Green, which aims at saving 20% of energy at data center operation through the integration of an energy aware management plug-in on top of the existing data center framework system[1]. Multi-agent frameworks supporting distributed resource constrained scheduling problems [7,8] are considered as an alternative for improved workload control, which can lead to shaping of energy load. Increasing flexibility in contracting between DCs and ICT end-users, and exchanging energy demand and supply information between energy producers and DCs allows more energy-efficient power management at DCs and at the same time meeting Green-SLAs.

SLA as a mean to actively influence the environmental impact of DC operation has not been thoroughly tackled in research. Some preparatory work ([11]) has been carried on in the in the area of SLA-based scheduling with the goal to evade SLA breaches by turning them into scheduling algorithms [4]. The power of SLA for environmental objectives has been first recognized by [5] where new SLA parameters trying to catch the CO2 impact of DC operation were introduced and approach comparable to [3] who integrated CO2 parameters into the quasi-standard for scientific SLA, the WS-Agreement. The concept of GreenSLA was introduced by [1], [2] in the context of energy efficient DC operation.

3 Establishing a Collaboration between Energy Provider, Data Center and End User

3.1 Energy Provisioning

The Smart Grid is supposed to lead us into an energy efficient era with less overhead in energy production, less wasted energy on the consumer side, and an increased utilization of renewable energy. However, the combined volatility of both, energy supply and energy demand leads to a major challenge: On the one hand, high demands of energy (imposed at peak times) result in the activation of less efficient energy generation. On the other hand, renewable energies are unfortunately based on energy sources that tend to be subject to uncontrollable factors as, e.g., wind or sunlight, and need to be consumed as available.

Energy production can be classified into base load, medium load, peak load, and renewable energy generation (see figure 1) which have different characteristics regarding the dynamic adaptation to volatility of demand. These characteristics, in turn, have different impact on CO2 emissions and power density[2]:

- Peaking power plant:
  - Generation of energy is very expensive and resource intensive (mostly fossil energy sources)

---

[1] http://www.fit4green.eu/

[2] In the first project phase, CO2 will be the main indicator to assess the impact of the energy conversion process on the environment. However, this measure doesn't capture e.g. the potential risk of nuclear energy. Therefore one research topic is to integrate other output measures into the CO2 indicator.

- Highly responsive to changes in load
- Pumped-storage hydroelectricity, gas turbines

– Medium load power plant:
  - Medium cost for energy generation
  - Responsiveness to changes in load is moderate
  - Combined gas and steam power plants

– Renewable energy sources:
  - Replaces energy sources for base load
  - Wind and solar power

– Base load power plant:
  - Cheap and relatively efficient generation of energy
  - Responsiveness to changes in load is low
  - Nuclear, coal, hydro power

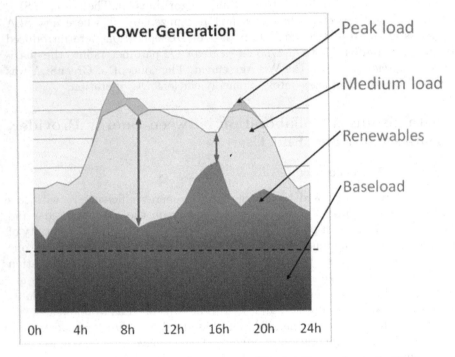

Fig. 1. Structure of power generation (Source: Brautsch et al., 2011)

Generally speaking, the quicker the power plants have to react to energy demand spikes, the greater the impact on the environment. The peaking power as the most flexible and least environmentally desirable is generated whenever the energy demand exceeds the planned limit. Today it is exclusively up to the EP (who can also be a producer, an energy trader or a mix of the two roles) to react to sudden increase in energy demand by adding inefficiently produced peak energy to the grid. The potential for closer interaction between energy producers and energy users like DCs is thus not tapped.

3.2   The All4Green Eco-system

In this section, the infrastructure of the grid proposed by All4Green project is presented. Instead of putting the focus of the energy optimization in DCs solely on ICT resources and/or HVAC infrastructure within the DC, All4Green broadens the scope and integrates all players into one eco-system. Within this eco-system, the DC or DC Federation (denoted DCF) has the double role of being the customer of the EP as well as being the supplier of ICT services to their customers. EU/End User represents the demand side of the DC. A typical user aims at minimizing the total costs of computing, i.e. the price paid to DC for computing services, but also has a bias to choose for SLAs that provide more sustainable and more energy-efficient energy usage. It will prefer cheaper, longer term contracts, providing stability for computing services; contracts with DCs with a better reputation, e.g. based on "good history"; contracts which provide better service levels, i.e. higher quality, less execution delays and fewer incidents, and those less binding, i.e., the ones which allow de-commitment without penalties from EU's part but not from DC's part. User propensity for green computing and Green SLAs will encourage DCs that are able to provide Green Computing using renewable energy sources. EP/Energy Provider represents the energy supply side for the DC. Its goals are to acquire a uniform and predictable load for all energy delivered to DC, and in some countries to not exceed its maximum amount of emissions, i.e. a "Green Quota" established by the Government. It tries to apply different strategies to maximize its profit while selecting the most preferred and easily available energy source mix from its suppliers. This is why EP prefers predictable energy loads and uses energy consumption profiles of its DC customers, shared voluntarily as part of energy provisioning agreements, or measured by EP based on monitored Key Performance Indicators. In order to reduce cost, EP tries to avoid power peaks, as this is traditionally the most costly power and involving non-renewable energy sources.

DC/Data Center acts as provider of computing services and as demand side for the EP. With its specific business model it wants to stay on the market, maximizing turnover, minimizing cost. One sustainability strategy can be to market green products. The DC's workload profile influences its energy consumption profile and it can choose to share this profile with the EP to obtain a discounted energy price for a given energy source provisioned by EP. The DC also employs forecasting to anticipate its own workload profile under different strategies for accepting computing requests.

Figure 2 shows the envisioned relations between the EP, the DCs and the ICT EUs. The communication between the EP and its customers (e.g., the DCs) will be bidirectional, instead of just unidirectional, as it is now. Nowadays, in general there is no (or just a very limited) digital communication between these entities, and the EP only has knowledge about the overall amount of power that was consumed in the past. Thus, the possibilities to send data from the EP to the customers (and vice versa) are very limited. However, for a smart, ecological grid, this is a crucial requirement, since an intelligent distribution and well-planned scheduling of available power resources is not possible without further

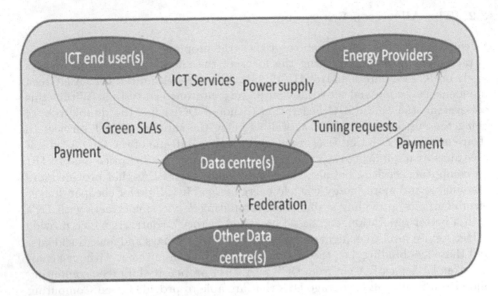

Fig. 2. All4Green Eco-System

information about the customer's future needs. Customers that agree to delay some power-consuming tasks for some hours have to be noticed in case that enough energy gets available inside the grid, so they can start their tasks. Of course, the EP cannot send the same signal to all its customers. Otherwise, too many participants might start consuming energy at the same time so that the demands for energy would overwhelm the currently available resources. So, a scheduling approach has to be developed to notify the right subset of consumers at the right time. Additional information about the delayed tasks and the amount of energy a customer usually needs at a specific time of day should be taken into account by the EP.

For this, a digital connection between DC and EP is needed

- to send notifications regarding available energy resources from the energy provider to the DC.
- to send notifications from the EP to the DC in case there is an energy shortage in the grid and to ask the customer to reduce its consumption.
- to tell the EP which amount of energy will be needed in the near future and for how long. Additional information that supports scheduling could also be included, e.g., how urgently the energy will be needed then.
- to tell the EP how much energy is locally buffered (e.g. by the UPS) and could possibly be used by the data center itself (e.g., by switching off the UPS as backup-energy or as energy storage in case the grid state is getting critically low/high).

For planning purposes, up-to-date information will be needed. This gets even more important when renewable energy sources should be used by the providers.

Short-term fluctuations of the amount of produced power complicate the prediction of available energy. To deliver energy in a timely manner to its customers, the EP also needs to receive up-to-date information from the customers.

Scheduling is not only done by the EP. Inside a DC, some non-urgent tasks can be delayed. Another way of raising or reducing the amount of needed energy is to migrate workload to federated DCs located in, e.g., another country or region. For instance, tasks are moved to a place where enough energy is currently available - meaning: It is more energy efficient to move jobs to where they can be done, instead of moving energy to where it is needed.

Furthermore, a DC that hosts workload for its ICT EUs, might introduce a new kind of green contracts (GreenSLAs, see section 4.2). EUs that agree to accept a limited QoS reduction for their hosted services might get better pricing conditions.

4   Strategies for Shaping the Energy Demand in Data Centers

There are several energy saving techniques that have been successfully applied in DCs [10] and amongst others can be used to shape the demand in a DC or a DCF in order to comply with requests from an EP. Additionally, in order to exploit the full potential of the envisioned collaborative approach, economic incentives are being developed that foster the collaboration between DC and EU and also instigate the cooperation between DC and EP.

4.1   All4Green Energy Shaping Techniques

This section contains several techniques for energy load shaping in a DC.

Dynamical Server consolidation. A dynamic measure to reduce energy consumption is to consolidate servers that are not used at their normal capacity into fewer ones, with a better utilization. Thus freed, unused servers can be shut down. When load will grow, some of these servers will be restarted (FIT4Green approach) [12] [13].

Server Virtualization. Virtualization helps consolidate workload on fewer physical servers.

Workload migration across a federation of data centers. The solution of workload migration is particularly interesting when the transfer of tasks takes place between geographically dispersed nodes, which are subject to different geographical characteristics (cold vs. warm climate) and availability of energy sources (wind power instead of coal).

Other techniques. The main problem faced by DC is a dynamic workload demand with abrupt peaks of energy consumption, followed by lower than average demand (outside working hours, at night and during week-ends). Through adapting mid-term workload planning to energy supply planning, peaks can be avoided.

Cooling. The cooling infrastructure can serve as energy buffer: At times of high energy supply (through wind, sun) the temperature in the DC can be reduced beyond what is necessary. This buffer can be utilized in times of scares energy. Moreover, thermal "debts" can be created by allowing the temperature to rise up to a certain extent these debts can then be paid back with renewable energy.

UPS. In the event of power shortages or even periods of energy peaks, Uninterruptible Power Systems (UPS) can be started. They can function for systems independently or in parallel with EP power-generating system, for as long as the energy provided by EP is insufficient for all active servers and virtual machines at DC, and after the energy consumption peak is over, they can be stopped again.

Negotiation as workload coordination mechanism. The actors in the DC ecosystem can participate in a multi-party negotiation to shape the energy demand in the DC. Separate DC-EP and DC-EU negotiations can take place, with different frequencies and for different objectives: DC-EP negotiation take place weekly or monthly to establish the energy source mix and price per KWh that the DC needs to pay to EP (based on the average energy load demand in the previous period, and the stability/uniformity of the consumption profile). DC-EU negotiations take place monthly or periodically as agreed upon in the SLA and aim at establishing the maximum computing delays for a given computing task cost.

4.2   All4Green Energy Shaping Incentives

The technical collaboration approach introduced above offers a high potential for the optimization of energy provision. Within the traditional legal and economic boundaries however, this potential remains untapped to a great degree: On the one hand full elasticity of electricity supply between EP and DC has been an undisputed principle until now, on the other hand strict performance guarantees between DCs and their customers limit the scope for energy shaping measures in the DC.

This is why All4Green explores strategies that aim at economically supporting the technical options offered by the collaboration tool. A powerful leverage to do this are the contracts between EP and DC as well as between DC and EUs.

There is a bundle of different energy tariffs a business can choose from for the contract with its EP. Most of these are a combination of a baseline tariff that depends on the connected power and a variable component that depends on the kWh consumed.

In All4Green however this rationale of elastic supply is inverted: The EP needs options to require the collaboration from the DC in clearly specified boundaries. This calls for new energy tariffs that foster this collaboration by giving the EP the right to trigger energy shaping activities at the site of the DC. Such a contract will contain the definition of triggering events, but also limitations for the EP, for instance with regard to the number of triggering events per week or month and with regard to magnitude of the DCs activities. At the same time the contract must offer a trade-off for the DC, most likely in the form of a novel pricing system that connects the DC's electricity cost to the intensity of the realized collaboration thus rewarding the DC if it reacts positively to the triggering event.

However, also on the side of the DC, the scope of technical cooperation is limited due to performance guarantees the data center has given to its customers through their contracts. The guarantees between DC and customer are contained in the service level agreements (SLA), which are the technical parts of IT service contracts.

Until recently these SLA were biased toward sheer performance and availability orientation, no matter at what cost for the natural environment. This resulted for instance in SLAs based on the TIER I-IV categories that guarantee a certain standard of access (e.g. 24-7-365) and infrastructure redundancy. For certain applications, be it mission critical prototype test or medical simulations, performance will always be the most important requirement. There are other applications, however, that are not critical in the same way, be it regularly done back-up jobs or the processing of monthly billing data in a company. For these, in the context of All4Green, GreenSLA will be offered that trade the possibility of slight performance degradation against e.g. monetary incentives and a certified "greenness" of the IT service.

To this end, we define a GreenSLA as a SLA between a service provider and its customers that offers an extended scope for energy shaping measure to the service provider

- by replacing traditional performance parameters through allowed performance scopes
- by introducing novel energy performance parameters as classifying elements,
- keeping track of collaboration efforts from both DC and end-customer, and
- by offering incentives to the customers to agree to performance modifications and collaboration.

If a customer of a bank, e.g., agrees to such a GreenSLA, the fees for her bank account will be reduced at the expense of an increased waiting time for bank services like transferring money etc.This concept was first introduced in the context of energy saving measures in DCs [1],[2]. In All4Green it will be used in a different way not only helping to reduce the energy consumed by DCs without caring for adaptation processes at the EP's site, but by supporting the DC in actively shaping its energy demand: the goal "reduce energy consumption originating in costumer/applications specified in GreenSLA" is replaced by the goal "support DC's energy shaping efforts" under certain performance constraints.

5   Impact

All4Green aims at reducing the energy consumption accountable to the DC industry through a really upheaval approach. This is an objective which in turn, if reached, may significantly benefit the global energy consumption picture. As a matter of fact, in 2008 the European DC consumption was estimated at 50

TWh, expected to rise to 100TWh by 2020, roughly the same as the electricity consumption of Portugal. So, the project targets an area where obtaining results can have a relevant impact on overall sustainability.

Up to date, the energy saving (or emission saving) goals have been pursued through sectorial approaches, where each of the involved actors put forth its own instruments and action plans, looking at a reduction of its own consumption which didn't take into account nor tried to exploit the interactions with the other players of the DC supply chain. Nevertheless, acting in self-standing way can't avoid the occurrence of boundary and/or abnormal operation conditions, which, even if transient, can have a significant negative impact on the big energy consumption picture. Demand peaks are one of the most common and simple cases in point: peak energy conversion is ineffective ("rich" in CO2 and "poor" in efficiency terms). For instance, to produce 1MW from diesel fueled equipment (typically used during peak loads) requires approx. 250ltr/h, which means about 700 kg CO2 /h emission.

All4Green wants to minimize the negative impact of the above cases by developing technologies supporting an active cooperation among all the ecosystem actors (EPs, DC operators, and EUs), with the common purpose to control energy demand, and by this means obtain an overall energy saving around 10% for the system as a whole. This saving doesn't overlap with the ones you can achieve through self-standing improvements, on the contrary adds on to that, and can in general be applied even to ecosystems where ICT equipment, DC facilities and/or energy sources have not reached an intrinsic good level of efficiency yet.

A second positive effect of All4Green is to increase the percentage of renewable energy that can be fed into the electricity grid. Nowadays, to some degree due to their reduced constancy and predictability, solar or wind energy produced cannot be fully utilized because the power supply voltage is already at maximum. In Germany, for instance, a solar power plant with more than 100MW connection power is legally required to be detachable due to grid stability issues! Through the joint demand control mechanisms offered by All4Green, this problem can be much better tackled.

In terms of energy consumption management on the DC side, All4Green can positively impact two areas:

1. It can provide verifiable and transparent methods of measuring energy performance, by developing new metrics that encompass the whole value network aggregating ICT EU, DC and EP (and subsets thereof). These metrics will be developed in a way to show if the energy savings (triggered via technical changes, or economic incentives within the eco-system like Green-SLAs), materialize as real reductions of inputs of energy carriers into the technical and economic metabolism.
2. It can offer quantifiable and significant reduction of energy consumption and CO2 emissions, achieved through ICT. The reduction of energy consumption that can be achieved through ICT depends largely on:
   - The freedom DCs have in performing local optimizations by using Green-SLAs as contracts between ICT users and DCs. Inside ordinary DCs 10%

to 20% energy savings can be realized during certain time periods, particularly by DCs offering services to geographically concentrated users, on top of traditional strategies/policies already in place (that work with standard SLAs).

- The reduction of energy demand from non-renewable sources at the very beginning of the energy value chain: savings that can be transported to the origin of energy conversion are magnified from the environmental perspective. The collaboration between DC and power provider can result in a temporary 10%-20% reduction of the DC energy demand, typically by delaying or slowing down some activities, to help power providers manage energy consumption peaks.
- The ability to "migrate" workload across the DCF can reduce the transport needs of energy from remote providers, and thus avoid the 10% energy transport overheads.

If this vision is projected to all the European DCs (a very strong assumption), this would mean that through a well-working collaboration mechanism within the DC eco system, the huge amount of roughly 2000 t CO2e could be avoided by integrating the necessary energy consumption into the base or medium load instead of "producing" extra inefficient and dirty peak load energy which is about what 20.000 German families consume in those 2 hours!

6   Summary and Conclusions

This paper has presented a novel idea to face current and future problems caused by the ongoing energy transition. While more and more regenerative energy is produced and the production of nuclear power may be reduced in the future, new technologies are needed to keep the power grid stable.

The arising problems of energy production have been discussed in detail in this paper and the collaboration between energy producers, energy consumers, and finally their end-customers has been identified as feasible approach to customize energy demand with respect to the dynamic supply of energy. Especially, the energy-related eco-system of data centers has been looked at in detail, consisting of the energy provider, the data center and the end-customer of the data center. The paper has presented mechanisms as virtualization, consolidation, federation of data centers, and management of cooling systems and UPS that are able to achieve a high flexibility of energy demand within the data center. This flexibility can be used by the energy provider to adjust energy demand to the current availability of regenerative energy and to shave peaks in power demand to keep the power grid in a stable situation.

Furthermore, the paper has discussed incentives (as green SLAs) that are necessary to enable the needed collaboration within the energy-based eco-system of the data center. Finally the paper has discussed the possible impact of the suggested approach and presented the possible positive outcomes of the project All4Green.

Acknowledgments. This research has been carried out within the European Project All4Green (FP7-ICT-2011-6.2): www.all4green-project.eu. We acknowledge financial support from European Commission for project grant#288674 All4Green: Active collaboration in DC ecosystem to reduce energy consumption and GHG emissions.

References

1. Klingert, S., Bunse, C.: GreenSLAs for Energy Efficient Scheduling. In: Proceedings of the COST Action IC0804 on Energy Efficiency in Large Scale Distributed Systems - 2nd Year (2011)
2. Klingert, S., Schulze, T., Bunse, C.: Managing Energy-Efficiency by Utilizing GreenSLAs. In: Proceedings of E-Energy Conference 2011, New York (2011)
3. Lawrence, A., Djemame, K., Wäldrich, O., Ziegler, W., Zsigri, C.: Using Service Level Agreements for Optimising Cloud Infrastructure Services. In: Cezon, M., Wolfsthal, Y. (eds.) ServiceWave 2010 Workshops. LNCS, vol. 6569, pp. 38–49. Springer, Heidelberg (2011)
4. Sakellarriou, R., Yarmolenko, V.: Job Scheduling on the Grid: Towards SLA-Based Scheduling. In: Grandinetti, L. (ed.) High Performance Comp. and Grids in Action. Adv. in Parallel Comp., vol. 16 (2009)
5. Laszewski, G., Wang, L.: GreenIT Service Level Agreements. In: Grids and Service-Oriented Architectures for Service Level Agreements, pp. 77–88 (2010)
6. EPA Report to Congress on Server and Data Center Energy Efficiency Public Law 109-431, http://www.energystar.gov/ia/partners/prod_development/downloads/EPA_Datacenter_Report_Congress_Final1.pdf (last accessed: March 01, 2012)
7. Confessore, G., Giordani, S., Rismondo, S.: A market-based multi-agent system model for decentralized multi-project scheduling. Annals of Operations Research 150, 115–135 (2007)
8. The Green Grid Initiative. Project website, http://www.thegreengrid.org/ (last accessed March 01, 2012)
9. Basmadjian, R., Bunse, C., Georgiadou, V., Giuliani, G., Klingert, S., Lovasz, G., Majanen, M.: FIT4Green - Energy aware ICT Optimization Policies. In: Proceedings of the COST Action IC0804 on Energy Efficiency in Large Scale Distributed Systems (2010)
10. Buyya, R., Ranjan, R., Calheiros, R.N.: Modeling and Simulation of Scalable Cloud Computing Environments and the CloudSim Toolkit: Challenges and Opportunities. In: Proceedings of the 7th High Performance Computing and Simulation (HPCS 2009) Conference, Leipzig, Germany, June 21-24 (2009)
11. Basmadjian, R., Bunse, C., Georgiadou, V., Giuliani, G., Klingert, S., Lovasz, G., Majanen, M.: FIT4Green - Energy aware ICT Optimization Policies. In: Proc. Of the COST Action IC0804 on Energy Efficiency in Large Scale Distributed Systems - 1st Year. COST Office (2010), ISBN: 978-2-917490-10-5, http://www.irit.fr/cost8-..roceedings1styearworkshop
12. Lovasz, G., Niedermeier, F., De Meer, H.: Energy-Efficient Management of Physical and Virtual Resources - A Holistic Approach. In: Proc. of the COST Action IC0804 on Energy Efficiency in Large Scale Distributed Systems - 1st Year, pp. 80–83. COST Office (2010), ISBN: 978-2-917490-10-5, http://www.irit.fr/cost80..roceedings1styearworkshop

Modeling and Simulation of Data Center Energy-Efficiency in CoolEmAll

Micha vor dem Berge[1], Georges Da Costa[4], Andreas Kopecki[2], Ariel Oleksiak[3],
Jean-Marc Pierson[4], Tomasz Piontek[3], Eugen Volk[2], and Stefan Wesner[2]

[1] Christmann Informationstechnik + Medien
Micha.vordemBerge@christmann.info
[2] High Performance Computing Center Stuttgart
{kopecki,volk,wesner}@hlrs.de
[3] Poznan Supercomputing and Networking Center
{ariel,piontek}@man.poznan.pl
[4] IRIT, University of Toulouse
{georges.da-costa,pierson}@irit.fr

Abstract. In this paper we present an overview of the CoolEmAll project which addresses the important problem of data center energy efficiency. To this end, CoolEmAll aims at delivering advanced simulation, visualization and decision support tools along with open models of data center building blocks to be used in simulations. Both building blocks and the toolkit will take into account aspects that have major impact on actual energy consumption such as cooling solutions, properties of applications, and workload and resource management policies. In the paper we describe the CoolEmAll approach, its expected results and an environment for their verification.

Keywords: data centers, energy efficiency, simulations.

1 Introduction

Data centers are responsible for around 2% of the global energy consumption making it equal to the demand of aviation industry [8]. In many current data centers the actual IT equipment uses only half of the total energy (e.g. 45-62% in [2]) while most of the remaining part is required for cooling and air movement resulting in poor Power Usage Effectiveness (PUE) [23] values. Large energy needs and significant CO_2 emissions caused that issues related to cooling, heat transfer, and IT infrastructure location are more and more carefully studied during planning and operation of data centers. Even if we take ecological and footprint issues aside, the amount of consumed energy can impose strict limits on data centers. First of all, energy bills may reach millions euros making computations expensive. Furthermore, available power supply is usually limited so it also may reduce data center development capabilities, especially looking at challenges related to exascale computing breakthrough foreseen within this decade.

For these reasons many efforts were undertaken to measure and study energy efficiency of data centers. Some of projects focused on data center monitoring

J. Huusko et al. (Eds.): E²DC 2012, LNCS 7396, pp. 25–36, 2012.

and management [6][15] whereas others on prototypes of low power computing infrastructures [22]. Studies included aspects such as energy efficiency of
networks [16] and service level agreements related to energy consumption [17].
Additionally, vendors offer a wide spectrum of energy efficient solutions for computing and cooling [24][19][21]. However, a variety of solutions and configuration
options can be applied planning new or upgrading existing data centers. In order
to optimize a design or configuration of data center we need a thorough study
using appropriate metrics and tools evaluating how much computation or data
processing can be done within given power and energy budget and how it affects
temperatures, heat transfers, and airflows within data center. Therefore, there
is a need for simulation tools and models that approach the problem from a
perspective of end users and take into account all the factors that are critical to
understanding and improving the energy efficiency of data centers, in particular,
hardware characteristics, applications, management policies, and cooling.

To address these issues the CoolEmAll project [20] aims at decreasing energy
consumption of data centers by allowing data center designers, planners, and
administrators to model and analyze energy efficiency of various configurations
and solutions. To this end, the project will provide models of data center building
blocks and tools that apply these models to simulate, visualize and analyze data
center energy efficiency.

The structure of the paper is as follows. Section 2 contains a brief description
of the CoolEmAll project. In Section 3 we present the concept of open models of
data center building blocks which can be applied in simulations. In Section 4 the
main expected result of the project - the simulation and visualization toolkit - is
described. In Section 5 we show the environment for experiments and verification
of models and simulation tools. Section 6 concludes the paper.

2   The CoolEmAll Project

The main goal of CoolEmAll is to provide advanced simulation, visualization
and decision support tools along with blueprints of computing building blocks
for data centers. Once developed, these tools and blueprints should help to minimize the energy consumption, and consequently the CO_2 emissions of data centers. This will be achieved by: (i) design of diverse types of computing building
blocks well defined by hardware specifications, physical dimensions, and energy
efficiency metrics, and (ii) development of simulation, visualization and decision support toolkit (SVD Toolkit) that will enable analysis and optimization of
IT infrastructures built of these building blocks. Both building blocks and the
toolkit will take into account aspects that have major impact on actual energy
consumption: hardware characteristics, cooling solutions, properties of applications, and workload and resource management policies. To achieve it, the energy
efficiency of computing building blocks will be precisely defined by a set of metrics expressing relations between the energy efficiency and essential factors listed
above. In addition to common static approaches, the CoolEmAll platform will
enable studies of dynamic states of data centers based on changing workloads,

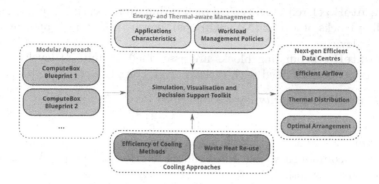

Fig. 1. The CoolEmAll concept

management policies, cooling method, and ambient temperature. The main concept of the project is presented in Figure 1.

The models and simulations tools will be verified using an environment presented in Section 5. The testing environment will be based on the RECS system [3] allowing fine grained monitoring and control. The next two sections contains descriptions of the main project expected results: data center building blocks and the SVD Toolkit.

3 Definition of Data Center Building Blocks

As mentioned, one of the main results of the CoolEmAll project will be the design of diverse types of datacenter building blocks on different granularity levels, following a blueprint-specification format called Data center Efficiency Building Block (DEBB). The following subsections describe the DEBB concept and design of the rack level datacenter building block called ComputeBox.

3.1 Data Center Efficiency Building Block (DEBB)

A DEBB is an abstract description of a piece of hardware and other components reflecting a data-center building block on different granularity levels. These granularities reach from a single node up to a complete data center and will help users to model a virtual data center for e.g. planning or reviewing processes. Within CoolEmAll, a DEBB can be described on following granularity levels:

1. **Node Unit** reflects the finest granularity of building blocks to be modeled within CoolEmAll. This smallest unit reflects a single blade CPU module, a so-called "pizza box", or a RECS CPU module.
2. **Node Group** reflects an assembled unit of building blocks of level 1, e.g. a complete blade center or a complete RECS unit (currently consisting of 18 node-units).

3. **ComputeBox1** reflects a typical rack within an IT service center, including building blocks of level 2 (Node Groups), power supply units and integrated cooling devices.
4. **ComputeBox2** building blocks are assembled of units of level 3, e.g. reflecting a container filled with racks or even complete compute rooms.

A DEBB on each granularity level is described by:

- Specification of components and sub-building blocks,
- Outer physical dimensions (black-box description), and optionally arrangements of components and sub-building blocks within particular DEBB (white-box description),
- Power consumption for different load-levels concerning mainly CPU and memory, and optionally IO and storage,
- Thermal profile describing air-flow (including direction and intensity) and temperature on inlets and outlets for different load-levels,
- Metrics describing energy efficiency of a DEBB.

As the focus of CoolEmAll is to simulate thermal behavior of a DEBB to enable design of energy efficient building blocks, it will be modeled as the smallest unit in the thermodynamic modeling process. As such, the complete Node Unit is the smallest feature that will be present in a simulation. The thermodynamic processes within a Node Group are only coarsely modeled as they are merely interesting for providing boundary conditions for the ComputeBox1 and ComputeBox2 simulations. The ComputeBox1 simulations will require – besides the arrangement of the Node Groups – the velocity field and temperature at the Node Group outlets over time as inbound boundary condition and will provide the room temperature over time at the outlet of the Node Group as outgoing boundary condition.

3.2   ComputeBox

In CoolEmAll we defined a first draft of a ComputeBox1 which is a bundle of pre-configured and ready-to-use components to deliver a complete data center in one rack [18]. Later on we will also define a blueprint of a ComputeBox2 which will have an even higher level of integration. The ComputeBox2 will be of the size of a container, whereas the ComputeBox1 has the size of a rack and will be described here briefly.

The main components of the ComputeBox1 are a special 19" rack with an integrated cooling solution, a monitoring architecture to be always aware of every important detail of the ComputeBox such as temperatures and power consumption of all components. Furthermore it will contain high-density and energy-efficient servers, which will be the RECS Multi-Node Computer in the CoolEmAll testbed case. In general, other systems would also be possible to be the basis for evaluation, but the RECS Computer system offers not only high energy-efficiency and density, but also an integrated high capable monitoring and controlling solution which enables us to monitor the complete rack at a very fine granularity without a negative impacting to the computing and network resources. A central and very fast storage will also be integrated and connected via a fast interconnect which is coincidently the backbone for the computing nodes.

4   Simulation, Visualization and Decision Support Toolkit

The main result of the CoolEmAll project will be the development of a simulation, visualization, and decision support toolkit (SVD Toolkit) for analysis and design of data centers. This platform will support IT infrastructure designers, decision makers and administrators in the process of planning new infrastructures or improving the existing ones. The platform will enable the optimisation of both the IT infrastructure design and operation. A modular approach to these simulations (according to modules defined in Section 3) provides many extension possibilities and a high level of customisation. CoolEmAll will develop a flexible simulation platform integrating models of applications, workload scheduling policies, hardware characteristics, cooling as well as air and thermal flows using computational fluid dynamics (CFD) simulation tools. Advanced visualization tools and user interfaces will allow users to easily analyse various options and optimise energy efficiency of planned data centers. The toolkit will also support users to realise a thermal- and energy-aware workload scheduling and resource management. The main CoolEmAll outcomes will be based on existing technologies, which are extended appropriately to meet the objectives. Thus, a main focus when designing the toolbox are the features already provided by possible integration candidates.

4.1   Architecture

The aim of the SVD Toolkit is to offer a cost effective, open solution for assessing the cooling needs of a data center. Different simulation modules will be brought together to deliver a flexible framework. Simulations integrated into the toolkit include CFD simulations for assessing the air condition of the rack or computing room. Workload simulations will provide estimated heat generation information for the CFD simulation. Various hierarchies will be modeled, ranging from single nodes and racks to well defined container-based Compute Boxes or full data center rooms. Figure 2 shows the workflow for analysis of the estimated compute room conditions and the parameters that determine the results. For creating a flexible workflow, a modular, extensible system has to be used. Therefore the orchestrator for the SVD Toolkit is the Simulation and Visualization platform COVISE [12]. It is used to steer the simulations included into the SVD Toolkit and to provide state of the art visualization for its results. COVISE is a modular and collaborative post-processing, simulation and visualization framework enabling the analysis of complex data sets in engineering and science. While COVISE is responsible for the data processing workflow, the main part of the work is done by the simulation and pre-processing modules that are part of it. In COVISE, an application is divided into several processing steps, which are represented by COVISE modules. These modules, being implemented as separate processes, can be arbitrarily spread across different heterogeneous machine

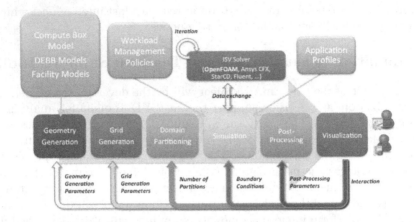

Fig. 2. Simulation workflow in the SVD Toolkit

platforms. The simulations run on separate high performance resources, while the SVD Toolkit itself can be run from a local workstation. This allows analysis of the results even with limited local hardware resources and enabling service based approach as mode of operation.

4.2 Workload Simulations

As said before, the goal of the SVD toolkit is to enable interactive analysis of data centers with respect to various important aspects that may affect their energy efficiency. One of these aspects is workload to be executed in a data center. Depending on its type, priority, and intensity a data center may consume different amounts of energy as well as diverse energy saving methods can be applied. To this end, CoolEmAll will take into consideration various workloads both from HPC and Cloud domain coming from HPC and data centers managed by organizations participating in the project. Applications running with and without virtualization will be studied.

In order to simulate workloads and workload scheduling policies the CoolE-mAll Data Center Workload Simulator will be developed. It will enable experimenting with different kinds of workloads and analyzing impact of scheduling and resource management policies on resource utilization and power usage. Within the SVD Toolkit the simulator will provide load and heat generation information for CFD simulations and visualization within SVD Toolkit. The simulator will be based on the GSSIM simulator [1], which will be extended by needed metrics and hardware models according to CoolEmAll requirements and SVD Toolkit integration needs. GSSIM already supports basic energy efficiency modeling features [9] and provides mechanisms to insert custom workloads and scheduling policies [10]. The simulation environment will also include means to insert application-specific performance and energy consumption models. More details concerning application modeling is presented in the next section.

4.3   Application Modeling, Profiling: Towards Adapted Benchmarks

The best way for a future user to evaluate the SVD Toolkit or a physical data center is to execute its own applications in these environments. Due to the unlimited number of possible applications, it is impossible to evaluate DEBBs and the SVD Toolkit using all of them. Therefore, the classical approach is to use representative benchmarks to give a good hint of quality. Alas, current knowledge of most scientific application concerns solely their performance (e.g. FLOPS for HPC and time to result or requests/second for services in industry). Hence classical benchmarks create differentiated behaviors performance-wise but their profile of power consumption and thermal impact is mainly unknown. To complete metrics with power consumption and thermal impact, several challenges are to be overcome :

- The first one is to be able to evaluate for any application its power consumption and heat production. It is particularly difficult due to the complexity of the running environment. While it is quite easy to evaluate the slowdown from having two applications on the same physical host, it is much more difficult to assess the power consumption at the application level. How to measure the relative power consumption of two applications[5] on the same physical host when the only way to measure this power is by using a wattmeter for the complete host is an open question. The same question emerges for the thermal impact which is based on a combination of power and time, as most applications have a non constant behavior over time.
- The second one is to be able to classify in the multi-dimentional impact space (performance, power, thermal) a handful of unique (but yet representative) applications that can serve as a basis for benchmarks. To achieve such a classification, the ability to recognize phases of application[4] during run-time is necessary in order to acquire the knowledge leading to the classification.

4.4   Heat Transfer Simulations

For assessing heat issues in a Compute Box or computing room, the heat dissipation and distribution of the nodes and its components have to be known. Heat generated by the compute nodes will be determined using the workload simulations based on earlier tests and application models. It is the task of the compute room cooling to dispose of the heat generated. The cooling devices in operation nowadays are most of the time air or fluid based, thus simulations concerned with the modeling of heat transfer and fluid dynamics can be used to assess the effectiveness of the cooling and to predict the room temperature distribution. For CoolEmAll an OpenFOAM [13] based solver will be integrated into the SVD Toolkit. OpenFOAM is not a complete and closed simulation package. Rather it is a C++ toolbox for the development of specific numerical solvers. It is maintained and released as open source under the GNU General Public License. OpenFOAM is a mature library for creating a large variation of solvers for many purposes. With using OpenFOAM, CoolEmAll is able to deliver assessment of the cooling for the computing nodes in an advanced and cost effective manner.

4.5   Visualization

To facilitate insight into the conditions within the compute room or rack it is necessary to post-process and visualize the data generated by the simulation in an appropriate manner. Fortunately, COVISE already includes extensive visualization capabilities that can be used to an advantage. All necessary post-processing steps can be included into the simulation workflow for immediate analysis (Figure 3). The simulation progress will be constantly monitored even while the simulation is running. The in-situ approach allows early assessments of the simulation results and shortens the evaluation cycles. COVISE visualization results can be explored on the desktop or in Virtual Reality, as well as on mobile devices. It is also possible to use Augmented Reality techniques to compare the simulation results with actual experimental data.

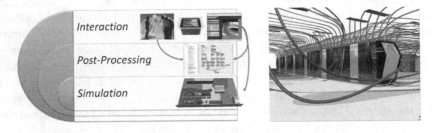

Fig. 3. Simulation, post-processing and interaction in one workflow

5   Verification Environment

To ensure the accuracy of models and simulations within the SVD Toolkit their elements have to be based and verified on experiments performed with the use of a real infrastructure. To address this issue a set of services and tools called Module Operation Platform (MOP) was designed to facilitate the phase of gathering measurements being an input for building models in SVD Toolkit and then to verify the proposed models and workload scheduling policies on real infrastructure. The MOP will be in charge of a vertical integration of the testbed components to enable operations such as fine grained monitoring and control as well as execution of experiments needed to perform aforementioned verifications. The system will be able to run both synthetic (generated by the Workload Generator Tool) and real workloads both for HPC and cloud case as indicated in Section 4.2. To perform repeatable experiments in an easy way, MOP will also include a repository of workloads, applications and benchmarks. Monitoring and controlling functionality of MOP will be available through web GUI including 3D visualization, which will enable comparison of real data with simulation results. The IT equipment used for the testbed, the monitoring and control layer, and evaluation metrics are briefly described in the following subsections.

5.1   RECS Multi-node Computer

The CoolEmAll testbed will be based on the RECS Multi-Node Computer (RECS) [3]. One highlight of the RECS is the very high density of 18 single server nodes within one Rack Unit which are at the date of this paper up to Intel i7 Quad-Core CPUs with 16 GB of RAM each. To enable the user to have a fine-grained monitoring- and controlling-system, the RECS has a dedicated master-slave system of microcontrollers integrated that can gather different metrics directly without the need of polling every single node or the need of Operation System support [6]. This enables us in the CoolEmAll project to gather many metrics like power usage, status and temperature for every node via only one request. The main advantage of this integrated monitoring system is to avoid the significant overhead which would be caused by measuring and transferring data on Operation system layer, which would consume lots of computing capabilities, particularly in a large-scale environment.

This microcontroller-based monitoring architecture can be accessed by users via a dedicated network port at the front of the server enclosure. To get all the information about the installed computing nodes, it has to be read out only once. The following example shows the immense capabilities of this approach. When a user monitors 10 metrics on all 18 nodes, he would have to perform 180 pulls, which can now be reduced to only one. Additionally, the master microcontroller that first collects all information from the different slave microcontrollers, can consolidate and filter the monitoring data. The RECS System is completely discless and thus needs some infrastructure servers to boot images. Via a central image- and boot-server all nodes can boot different types of images which can be changed very quickly. Through this infrastructure we reach a high flexibility to run different types of setups and tests for our project.

5.2   Monitoring and Controlling Infrastructure

The monitoring and controlling infrastructure of MOP is responsible for monitoring, data-history building, and controlling a hardware testbed on which experiments will be executed. Its architecture is based on the architecture of the TIMaCS framework [25], as described in [14]. The TIMaCS framework is designed as a policy based monitoring and management framework with an open architecture and a hierarchical structure, working on top of existing monitoring solutions, such as Nagios, Ganglia and others. The monitoring tools are collecting monitoring data from all compute nodes of the RECS, as well as from all RECS microcontrollers. Collected data is transformed into a uniform metric format then, and is aggregated and stored in a round robin database of the TIMaCS node, creating a data history that reflects a time-spatial behavior of captured metrics. Stored monitoring data can be retrieved and processed by MOP GUI or SVD Toolkit, allowing to analyze and correlate monitoring data with the simulation results.

Experiments executed on the testbed are determined by predefined workloads and management policies, controlled by *resource access and workload execution* service of MOP. For this purpose, *resource access and workload execution* service uses a batch system to submit and execute HPC jobs on predefined nodes, or a cloud-platform to deploy and execute VMs with cloud services. To enable controlling of resources, each managed resource is equipped with Delegates, interfaces allowing to execute commands on managed resources. *Resource access and workload execution* service uses these Delegates to set or change hardware parameters according to predefined policies.

5.3   Evaluation Metrics

Characterization of DEBBs in terms of energy efficiency is related to the CoolE-mAll metrics. These will find their foundation on previous works on energy related metrics [11] and Green Performance Indicators (GPIs), as defined in FP7 GAMES project [7]. GPIs are classified in four clusters: IT Resource Usage, Energy Impact, plus Organization GPIs (overall green involvement at organizational and business level), and Application Lifecycle KPIs (Key Performance Indicators, measuring response time, throughput, availability,...). We will focus on the two first clusters. IT Resource Usage GPIs characterize IT resource usage of applications and their environment. The energy consumption of an application service is characterized by its resource utilizations : CPU, memory, I/O, or even metrics related to space and performance (Space Watts and Performance - SWaP). Energy Impact GPIs describe the impact of IT service centers and applications on the environment considering power supply, consumed materials, emissions, and other energy related factors. These include application performance indicators (FLOPS/watts, transaction/watt), infrastructure related metrics (PUE, DCiE), compute power efficiency (CPE), coefficient performance of the ensemble (COP Ensemble) assessing the efficiency of the cooling. Linking Energy Impact GPIs with IT Resource Usage and Application Lifecycle KPI is a key challenge. The correlation between these indicators is obvious but not easy to express in a generic way and to derive a model from them, at the different levels of the infrastructure.

Indeed IT Resource Usage GPIs and IT facilities metrics (PUE, DCiE) are related to the infrastructure instantaneous power consumption but they do not encompass the evolution of the running environment with the applications. To fit with real usage, metrics need to take into account the temporal dimension (energy is a factor of power and time, and hot spots can only be spotted using an analysis in space and time) and the dynamic of the runtime environment (i.e. temperature distribution, heat transfers and management). Those dynamic metrics are by definition obtained at run-time. To compute them, two steps are needed: (1) measuring the system productivity and utilization, and, at the same time, the energy flows (power consumption, cooling demands, heat dissipation) of the hardware using a precise monitoring infrastructure; and (2) the mathematical modeling of the relationship from these observations linking system work performances and energy requirements.

To sum up, we are actually working on the assessment of dynamic metrics that could describe how a given data center architecture built from DEBBs is behaving in terms of space and time under certain loads.

6   Conclusions

In this paper we presented an overview of CoolEmAll, the new project that addresses the important problem of energy efficiency in data centers. CoolEmAll takes advantage of the results achieved by other projects such as GAMES [6] and aims at delivering a set of innovative models as well as simulation and visualization tools that will enable unprecedented analysis of data center energy efficiency. CoolEmAll will go beyond evaluations limited to basic measures such as PUE and typical analysis focusing on average or maximum loads as data centers usually do not operate at full load all the time and load types differ between centers. Instead it will allow studying all the issues and their correlations that may impact energy consumption including types and parameters of applications, workload and resource management policies, hardware configuration, hot/cold isles design, and cooling systems settings. CoolEmAll models and simulations tools will be verified using an innovative testbed based on the RECS system enabling very fine grained efficient monitoring and rich re-configuration options. Contrary to most of existing tools which are closed systems with integrated simulation codes, the CoolEmAll SVD Toolkit along with data center building blocks will be an open framework enabling integration of various tools for workload simulation, CFD simulation, and visualization. Various users such as HPC centers administrators, SMEs dealing with hardware design or data center solutions, data center designers, and researchers will be able to use the CoolEmAll tools in order to study ways of improving energy efficiency of data centers.

Acknowledgements. The results presented in this paper are partially funded by the European Commission under contract 288701 through the project CoolEmAll, and by the Federal Ministry of Education and Research (BMBF) through the project TIMaCS.

References

1. Bak, S., Krystek, M., Kurowski, K., Oleksiak, A., Piatek, W., Weglarz, J.: GSSIM - a Tool for Distributed Computing Experiments. Scientific Programming 19(4), 231–251 (2011)
2. Hintemann, R., Fichter, K.: Materialbestand der Rechenzentren in Deutschland, Eine Bestandsaufnahme zur Ermittlung von Ressourcen- und Energieeinsatz, UBA, Texte, 55/2010 (2010)
3. Christmann: Description for Resource Efficient Computing System (RECS) (2009), http://shared.christmann.info/download/project-recs.pdf
4. Da Costa, G., Pierson, J.-M.: Characterizing Applications from Power Consumption: A Case Study for HPC Benchmarks. In: Kranzlmüller, D., Toja, A.M. (eds.) ICT-GLOW 2011. LNCS, vol. 6868, pp. 10–17. Springer, Heidelberg (2011)

5. Da Costa, G., Hlavacs, H., Hummel, K., Pierson, J.-M.: Modeling the Energy Consumption of Distributed Applications. In: Handbook of Energy-Aware and Green Computing. Chapman & Hall, CRC Press (2012)
6. Kipp, A., Schubert, L., Liu, J., Jiang, T., Christmann, W., vor dem Berge, M.: Energy Consumption Optimisation in HPC Service Centres. In: Topping, B.H.V., Ivanyi, P. (eds.) Proceedings of the Second International Conference on Parallel, Distributed, Grid and Cloud Computing for Engineering. Civil-Comp Press, Stirlingshire (2011)
7. Kipp, A., Jiang, T., Fugini, M., et al.: Layered Green Performance Indicators. Future Generation Computer Systems 28(2), 478–489 (2012)
8. Koomey, J.: Worldwide electricity used in data centers. Environmental Research Letters 3(034008) (September 23, 2008)
9. Krystek, M., Kurowski, K., Oleksiak, A., Piatek, W.: Energy-aware simulations with GSSIM. In: 1st Year Proceedings of the COST Action IC0804 (2010)
10. Kurowski, K., Oleksiak, A., Piatek, W., Weglarz, J.: Hierarchical Scheduling Strategies for Parallel Tasks and Advance Reservations in Grids. Journal of Scheduling 11(14), 1–20 (2011), doi:10.1007/s10951-011-0254-9
11. Pierson, J.-M.: Energy: A New Criteria for Performances in Large Scale Distributed Systems. In: Hummel, K.A., Hlavacs, H., Gansterer, W. (eds.) PERFORM 2010. LNCS, vol. 6821, pp. 38–48. Springer, Heidelberg (2011)
12. Wierse, A., Lang, U., Rühle, R.: A System Architecture for Data-Oriented Visualization. In: Lee, J.P., Grinstein, G.G. (eds.) Visualization-WS 1993. LNCS, vol. 871, pp. 148–159. Springer, Heidelberg (1994)
13. Weller, H.G., Tabor, G., Jasak, H., Fureby, C.: A tensorial approach to computational continuum mechanics using object-oriented techniques. Computers in Physics 12(6), 620–631 (1998)
14. Volk, E., Buchholz, J., Wesner, S., Koudela, D., Schmidt, M., et al.: Towards Intelligent Management of Very Large Computing Systems. In: Proceedings of the Competence in High Performance Computing 2010 (2012)
15. Berl, A., Gelenbe, E., di Girolamo, M., Giuliani, G., de Meer, H., Dang, M.-Q., Pentikousis, K.: Energy-Efficient Cloud Computing. The Computer Journal 53(7) (2010)
16. Gelenbe, E., Morfopoulou, C.: Power savings in packet networks via optimised routing. Mobile Networks and Applications 17(1), 152–159 (2012)
17. Klingert, S., Schulze, T., Bunse, C.: GreenSLAs for the Energy-efficient Management of Data Centres. In: 2nd International Conference on Energy-Efficient Computing and Networking, e-Energy (2011)
18. CoolEmAll Report D3.1: First definition of the flexible rack-level ComputeBox with integrated cooling, http://coolemall.eu
19. Colt Modular Data Centre, http://www.colt.net/uk/en/products-services/data-centre-services/modular-data-centre-en.html
20. The CoolEmAll project website, http://coolemall.eu
21. EcoCooling, http://www.ecocooling.org
22. The MontBlanc project website, http://www.montblanc-project.eu/
23. The Green Grid Data Center Power Efficiency Metrics: PUE and DCiE, http://www.thegreengrid.org/Global/Content/white-papers/The-Green-Grid-Data-Center-Power-Efficiency-Metrics-PUE-and-DCiE
24. SGI ICE Cube Air, http://www.sgi.com/products/data_center/ice_cube_air/
25. TIMaCS (Tools for Intelligent Management of very large Computing Systems) project website, http://www.timacs.de

SLAs for Energy-Efficient Data Centres: The Standards-Based Approach of the OPTIMIS Project

Wolfgang Ziegler

Fraunhofer Institute SCAI, 53754 Sankt Augustin, Germany
wolfgang.ziegler1@scai.fraunhofer.de

Abstract. In current Cloud environments customers aiming to select a provider that offers energy efficient infrastructure usually depend on believing in the providers' publicity. In general they have little chances to alter the standard contract the big providers are offering. Smaller providers might offer the possibility to include energy efficiency as a clause in their paper framework contract. However, so far there is no way to dynamically create a Service Level Agreement with a provider that includes a certain level of energy efficiency the provider guarantees. The European project OPTIMIS is focussing on optimisation of cloud infrastructure services meeting demands from service providers. Besides a number of other parameters like trust, risk, cost, data protection this also includes aspects of energy efficiency. We describe the standards-based approach of OPTIMIS for negotiating and creating Service Level Agreements between service providers and infrastructure providers regarding energy efficiency of a data centre.

1 Introduction

The European project OPTIMIS is addressing optimisation of cloud infrastructure services meeting demands from service providers (SP), e.g. when public and private Clouds are federated in different configurations. This optimisation considers trust, risk, eco-efficieny, cost (the TREC parameters), data protection and data security (as presented in [10]. We describe the standards-based approach of OPTIMIS for negotiating and creating Service Level Agreements between end-users or service providers and infrastructure providers regarding energy efficiency of a data centre.

So far, dynamic electronic Service Level Agreements (SLAs) are rarely used in Clouds to define and agree upon the QoS the infrastructure provider (IP) will deliver to its customers regardless whether the customer is an end-user or a SP providing its services to the end-user. Even worse, the standard SLA offered by providers covers resource properties and an expected uptime but does not include any aspects of energy efficiency of a data centre a customer could claim. Nevertheless, a number of activities in different standards bodies have produced standards or are on the way to produce a standard relevant in the area of Cloud

J. Huusko et al. (Eds.): E²DC 2012, LNCS 7396, pp. 37–46, 2012.

computing. The most relevant for SLAs on energy efficiency are briefly described in this paper along with those that could play a role when further extended. The focus of the following sections is the descriptions of the standards-based approach of OPTIMIS for negotiating and creating SLAs between IPs and SPs that include the energy efficiency level agreed upon between customer and provider. The OPTIMIS developments enable the customer to reach a binding agreement with the provider and support the provider in optimising its infrastructure with respect to energy efficiency.

The remainder of the paper is organised as follows. Section 2 presents related work. Section 3 highlights current activities in different standards bodies regarding Cloud-relevant standards. Section 4 discusses general aspects of Service Level Management (SLM), how SLM is used in OPTIMIS and the technology for creating the Service Level Agreements. Section 5 presents the life-cycle of the OPTIMIS SLAs. A discussion of the approaches followed in the project regarding integration of energy efficiency in the SLAs can be found in the following Section 6 presenting a static approach based on external certification and an approach based on calculated average rates in Section 6.1 and 6.2 respectively along with the corresponding term language in 6.3 and gives an outlook on work started recently to integrate real-time power consumption monitoring data into the OPTIMIS environment in 6.4. The paper concludes with a summary and plans for future work.

2   Related Work

Until now only limited research has been focusing on SLAs for Clouds. In [14] an approach for using SLA in a single cloud scenario is presented. In case of SLA violation a penalty mechanism is activated rather than dynamically extending the hardware resources provided as realised in OPTIMIS. Moreover, despite the fact the authors complain about missing standards in this area they propose using IBM's proprietary solution developed 7 years ago. In 2010 [4] addresses challenges for IaaS, identifying Service Level Agreements as one of them which attracted little attention so far. IBM recently published a review and summary of cloud service level agreements [8] as part of their Cloud Computing Use Cases Whitepaper [9], which suggests SLA requirements and metrics for Cloud environments. However, this is not linked to any concrete implementation. Finally, in the European RESERVOIR project [15] SLAs have been used to define and monitor QoS of services deployed in Cloud infrastructures but no QoS parameters related to the infrastructure the services have been deployed in has been covered by these SLAs. As of today, to our best knowledge there is no related work on using Service Level Agreements between a user or a SP and an IP to establish an electronic contract regarding the required level of energy efficiency of a data centre.

3   Standardisation Approaches

Cloud technology has entered the focus of a number of standardisation bodies over the last three years, e.g. NIST, IEEE, TeleManagement Forum, OASIS, DMTF. However, most often the work is still in an early phase and far from delivering implementable specifications. Exceptions are, e.g. the OCCI [12] and WS-Agreement [1] specifications of the open Grid Forum (OGF). The latter is defining language and a protocol for creating SLAs, which was already published May 2007. While having been developed in the context of Grid computing WS-Agreement Specification is domain agnostic and allows the usage of any domain specific or standard condition expression language to define SLOs. In 2011 it was complemented by WS-Agreement Negotiation [2][3], which offers a multi-step negotiation protocol on top of WS-Agreement. The second broadly used standard of the OGF is the Open Cloud Computing Interface (OCCI), which is used by a number of Cloud providers and Cloud middleware stacks as an open, interoperable interface. The Distributed Management Task Force (DMTF) published in 2009 version 1.0 of the Open Virtualisation Format (OVF) [13] specification. OVF provides a standard format for packaging and describing virtual machines and applications for deployment across heterogeneous virtualisation platforms, while the related profiles standardise many aspects of the operational management of a heterogeneous virtualised environment. In OPTIMIS OVF is used to describe disk images. More recently the Telemanagement Forum has started as working group on Cloud SLAs. IEEE has launched a standards activity related to cloud federation with its group P3202. The group has no plans yet for using SLAs for the federation process. In 2011 National Institute of Standards and Technology (NIST) published the NIST Cloud Computing Reference Architecture [11] and the NIST Cloud Computing Standards Roadmap [7], however so far Cloud SLAs are not included. Moreover, the OASIS TC on Topology and Orchestration Specification for Cloud Applications (TOACA) published in March 2012 the Committee Specification Draft [16] for the formal description of service templates used to specify the topology and orchestration of IT services. A WS-Agreement rendering is under discussion. Finally, in April 2012 several of the before mentioned organisations started a cross SDO working group to better understand, coordinate and integrate their respective work related to Cloud standards.

4   Service Level Management

OPTIMIS implements two phases for Service Level Management (SLM): (i) specification of the requirements an SP or its customer has with respect to the virtualised infrastructure, and (ii) negotiating and creating the SLA on these requirements between SP and IP.

SLAs represent contractual relationships between the SP and the IP. SLAs describe the infrastructure service that is delivered, the functional and non-functional properties of the service, and the obligations of each party involved.

Additionally, SLAs define guarantees for the functional and non-functional service properties. These guarantees specify a service level objective that must be met in order to fulfil a guarantee. Compensations in form of penalties and rewards may be linked with guarantees becoming due in case the guarantee is fulfilled or violated respectively. The OPTIMIS Cloud QoS (QoS) component responsible for the SLM is an extension of the WSAG4J framework [17], which is an implementation of WS-Agreement and WS-Agreement Negotiation realised at the Fraunhofer Institute SCAI. It provides comprehensive support for common SLA management tasks such as SLA template management, SLA negotiation and creation, and SLA monitoring and accounting.

5   Service Level Agreements

5.1   SLA Life-Cycle

The OPTIMIS SLAs have a fairly standard life cycle, which they are running through from the initial preparation of the templates for an agreement up the evaluation whether the agreement has been fulfilled, or partly or completely violated. SLA life-cycles typically look like decribed in [5] and consist of several phases; these phases are shown in Figure 1.

Fig. 1. SLA life-cycle

The activities in the individual phases can be described and mapped to the OPTIMIS toolkit components as shown below. Involved components are QoS, the SP's Service Deployment Optimiser (SDO) and the IP's Cloud Optimiser (CO).

1. *SLA Development:* In this phase the SLA templates are developed. In OPTI-MIS generic templates have been defined and are accessible from the service providers. After selecting the service provider based on the requirements in the service manifest (SM) the QoS component extends the generic template with the SM for further negotiation.
2. *Negotiation:* In this phase the SLA is negotiated and the contracts are executed. The QoS component negotiates with the IP's CO component
3. *Implementation:* where the SLA is generated. Triggered by the SP through the SDO, done by the QoS component in OPTIMIS.
4. *Execution:* The SLA is executed, monitored, and maintained. The QoS component provides an interface to subscribe to an information service where, e.g. the service provider can retrieve monitoring information during this phase.

5. *Assessment:* Evaluation of the SLA performance. In this phase, a re-evaluation of the initial SLA template might be done. This is done by the QoS component, the result can be retrieved by other OPTIMIS components, e.g. the SDO.

Additional transitions between the *Implementation* or the *Execution* phase back to the *Negotiation* phase can be performed when re-negotiation of an agreement is required.

After the agreement has been created it is possible to retrieve monitoring information on the states of the agreement terms. Based on the evaluation of the individual service term states it can be decided whether an agreement is still fulfilled or risks to be violated if no appropriate countermeasures are taken. The sequence diagram in Figure 2 depicts the general steps required for querying monitoring information from an agreement. Please note: in the OPTIMIS environment the *ServiceConsumer* is the SP and the *ServiceProvider* is the IP.

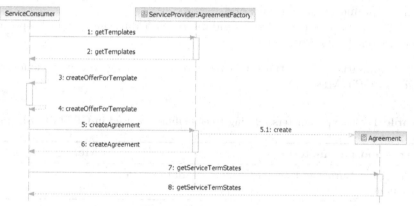

Fig. 2. SLA monitoring

6 Term Language for the Specification of Energy Efficiency Requirements

OPTIMIS follows three complementary approaches for assessing energy efficiency of the IP. The first year was focussing on certification regarding eco-efficiency. The current second year develops a model for breaking down the overall power consumption to average rates for Virtual Machines (VM) depending on classes of infrastructure the VMs are deployed to. The third year will finally develop proto-typical infrastructure to integrate real-time monitoring of power consumption.

6.1 Approach Based on Static Certification Information

In order to provide SLA-aware infrastructure services with extended QoS capabilities the SLA management layer requires capabilities to detect under-performing

with respect to the SLAs defined. However, in the case of static information regarding energy efficiency of a data centre we rely on external certifications currently available. Provider selection is done based on these properties, no monitoring is needed when the services are deployed in the data centre as these properties are not expected to change during a deployment.

The core measurable for eco-efficiency are **Energy** (in kilowatts per hour per VM) and **Carbon** (in kg CO_2 per hour per VM) associated with operational energy. In addition, there are a number of ways, beyond basic energy use, that datacenter operators can demonstrate eco-efficiency. The following already are used commonly:

- PUE (power usage effectiveness). This measures the infrastructure overhead of the facility and is a measure of the energy efficiency of the data centre (but not the IT equipment).
- Conformance to the EU Code of Conduct (COC) for data centers. This sets out best practices and operators must endorse the code or be a full signatory.
- Energy Star for data centres. This US driven certification of energy efficiency will be promoted across the world.
- LEED for data centres. This standard rates a datacenter for the positive impact on the environment.

Table 1 summarises the initial set of basic terms relating to eco-efficiency that are used in OPTIMIS SLAs.

Table 1. Basic parameters relating to eco-efficiency used in OPTIMIS SLAs

Terms and parameters	Metric
Is the centre European Code of Conduct for data centre compliant?	Yes/No
Does the centre have an Energy Star for data centre rating?	Points range or star rating, No
Is the centre LEED for data centre rated?	Platinum, Gold, Silver, Bronze, No

6.2   Approach Based on Availability of Specific Data Related to Energy Consumption and Carbon Footprint

For the second approach we are using the overall power consumption information of a data centre for a certain period (and corresponding CO_2 equivalent based on the local carbon content factor and any offsets or credits etc) already available for the infrastructure provider through the bills received from its electricity supplier. If not published, the CO_2 equivalent can be estimated from the region a data centre is located and the power supplier's technology used for electricity generation. Other sources for this information include, e.g. the annual reports of Greenpeace on data centres [6]. Based on this information further estimates can be made by the infrastructure provider to break the energy consumption and the CO2 emission down to an average rate per hour per VM instance. Of course, these calculations and their results also will need a certification by an independent institution to increase trustworthiness for customers. Providing this information to customers or brokers will allow taking the average rates into account when choosing the infrastructure provider. Further, the rates specified as requirements in the manifest become part of the SLA enabling the provider to check against internal measurements at run-time and to take counter measures in case of exceeding the values agreed upon. Corrective measures could be taken locally by the IP to avoid that the SLA is violated or - in case the provider realises that local countermeasures won't solve the problem - by migrating the service to another provider (after negotiating a new agreement that provides at least the same QoS level as the original SLA with the customer). Of course, initially only IPs that are part of the OPTIMIS consortium are ready to publish their average rates. However, we expect the situation will change over time when energy efficiency becomes a competitive factor for the IPs and SLAs with customers will include the requested energy efficiency level.

6.3   OPTIMIS Service Manifest

As mentioned before, we use the SM to describe the requirements regarding service QoS from the viewpoint of the SP or end-user. The following code exemplifies the part of the SM related to energy efficiency. The section consists of two parts. The first part specifies the requirements regarding static certification of an infrastructure provider as described in 6.1. The second part specifies requirements can be used used for infrastructure providers periodically publishing information allowing to assess their energy efficiency.

```
<opt:EcoEfficiencySection xmlns:opt="http://schemas.optimis.eu/optimis/">
    <opt:LEEDCertification>NotRequired</opt:LEEDCertification>
    <opt:BREEAMCertification>NotRequired</opt:BREEAMCertification>
    <opt:EuCoCCompliant>false</opt:EuCoCCompliant>
    <opt:EnergyStarRating>100</opt:EnergyStarRating>
```

In the section above the infrastructure provider's customer requests that the data-centre should have an Energy Star rating of 100. This could be verified before creating the SLA by accessing the Energy Star website, which would list the data centre once it has achieved the certification. However, currently there are no data centres listed there.

```
    <opt:EnergyConsumptionSection>
        <opt:AverageRatesPerVM>
            <opt:Large>
                <opt:EnergyConsumptionPerVm>
                    <opt:Electricity opt:unit="kWh">300</opt:Electricity>
                    <opt:Carbon opt:unit="kg">150</opt:Carbon>
                </opt:EnergyConsumptionPerVm>
```

```
        </opt:Large>
        <opt:Medium>
            <opt:EnergyConsumptionPerVm>
                <opt:Electricity opt:unit="kWh">200</opt:Electricity>
                <opt:Carbon opt:unit="kg">100</opt:Carbon>
            </opt:EnergyConsumptionPerVm>
        </opt:Medium>
        <opt:Small>
            <opt:EnergyConsumptionPerVm>
                <opt:Electricity opt:unit="kWh">100</opt:Electricity>
                <opt:Carbon opt:unit="kg">50</opt:Carbon>
            </opt:EnergyConsumptionPerVm>
        </opt:Small>
    <opt:AverageRatesPerVM>
</opt:EnergyConsumptionSection>
```

The section above specifies exemplifies the required average rates for the three types of VMs (large, medium, small, similar to Amazon's classification) plus the respective CO2 equivalent for a concrete data centre. A SP or a broker may use the average rates provided by different IPs to select the provider and the type of VM best suited for the service to be deployed while trying to minimise the power consumption and corresponding CO2 equivalent according to the request in the SM.

6.4 Approach Based on Availability of Real-Time Monitoring Data

For the third approach we will be using real-time monitoring information regarding actual power consumption (and the calculated corresponding local CO2 equivalent) of the infrastructure a service is deployed to. It should be noted that while the average power consumption per hour and VM could be similar across different data centres the local CO2 equivalent may differ significantly since it heavily depends on the providers' energy choices.

Members of the OPTIMIS consortium are currently equipping machines in two testbeds with off-the-shelf electricity meters to figure out how real-time measurements can be retrieved and stored in the monitoring database in a useful way. On the other hand, many providers are already gathering power consumption data, which is used internally to monitor and optimise infrastructure and cooling facilities. Having access to this data will allow to check against the values in the SLA and to take counter measures in case of exceeding the values agreed upon. Corrective measures could be taken by the IP to avoid that the SLA is violated or - in case the provider cannot fulfil the SLA - either by the IP or by the SP, e.g. migrating the service to another provider (after negotiating a new agreement). Initially, only a few IPs will be willing to expose their internal power monitoring to their customers. However, as with the second approach we expect the situation will change over time when energy efficiency becomes a competitive factor for the IPs and SLAs with customers will include the requested energy efficiency level. Requirements based on the availability of real-time monitoring data of power consumption will be included in manifest and SLAs in the third project year starting summer 2012.

7   Conclusions and Future Work

We presented the European OPTIMIS project's standards-based approach for SLM in a multi-cloud environment. The focus of the work described is on SLAs between end-user or SP and IP for user driven selection of data centres based on their energy efficiency and contractual guarantees. The SLA technology is based on WS-Agreement and WS-Agreement Negotiation using the Java implementation WSAG4J. Next steps of the OPTIMIS project are full integration with the cloud-providers' real-time monitoring of the energy consumption. In parallel we are preparing the publication of the term languages developed in OPTIMIS in the document series of the Open Grid Forum as an initial step to converge to standardised term languages. The SLA framework is already available for download [17]. The first version of the integrated OPTIMIS toolkit is available through the OPTIMIS website, yearly updates reflecting the progress of the toolkit will be published there.

Acknowledgements. Work reported in this paper has been co-funded by the European Commissions ICT programme in the FP7 project OPTIMIS under grant #257115 and by the German Federal Ministry of Education and Research in the D-Grid project under grant #01AK800A.

References

1. Andrieux, A., Czajkowski, K., Dan, A., Keahey, K., Ludwig, H., Nakata, T., Pruyne, J., Rofrano, J., Tuecke, S., Xu, M.: Web Services Agreement Specification (WS-Agreement). REC Recommendation, Open Grid Forum (2011), GFD.192 recommendation, http://www.ogf.org/documents/GFD.192.pdf
2. Battré, D., Brazier, F.M.T., Clark, K.P., Oey, M., Papaspyrou, A., Wäldrich, O., Wieder, P., Ziegler, W.: A proposal for WS-Agreement Negotiation. In: IEEE Grid 2010 Conference (2010)
3. Battré, D., Brazier, F.M.T., Clark, K.P., Oey, M., Papaspyrou, A., Wäldrich, O., Wieder, P., Ziegler, W.: Web Services Agreement Negotiation Specification (WS-Agreement Negotiation). P-REC Proposed Recommendation. Open Grid Forum (2011), GFD.193 proposed recommendation,
http://www.ogf.org/documents/GFD.193.pdf
4. Dawoud, W., Takouna, I., Meinel, C.: Infrastructure as a service security: Challenges and solutions. In: 2010 The 7th International Conference on Informatics and Systems (INFOS), pp. 1–8 (March 2010)
5. Sun, W., et al.: The Role of XML in Service Level Agreements Management. Network Management Research Center, Beijing. Jiaotong University, IEEE (2005)
6. How Clean is Your Cloud? Greenpeace report (April 2012),
http://www.greenpeace.org/international/Global/international/publications/climate/2012/iCoal/HowCleanisYourCloud.pdf

7. Hogan, M., Liu, F., Sokol, A., Tong, J.: NIST Cloud Computing Standards Roadmap – Version 1.0. Technical report, National Institute of Standards and Technology: NIST Cloud Computing Standards Roadmap Working Group (2011)
8. Review and summary of cloud service level agreements. Accessible on IBM's web-site, http://public.dhe.ibm.com/software/dw/cloud/library/cl-rev2sla-pdf.pdf
9. Cloud Computing Use Cases Whitepaper Version 4.0., http://www.scribd.com/doc/18172802/Cloud-Computing-Use-Cases-Whitepaper
10. Lawrence, A., Djemame, K., Wäldrich, O., Ziegler, W., Zsigri, C.: Using Service Level Agreements for Optimising Cloud Infrastructure Services. In: Cezon, M., Wolfsthal, Y. (eds.) ServiceWave 2010 Workshops. LNCS, vol. 6569, pp. 38–49. Springer, Heidelberg (2011)
11. Liu, F., Tong, J., Mao, J., Bohn, R., Messina, J., Badger, L., Leaf, D.: NIST Cloud Computing Reference Architecture. Technical report, National Institute of Standards and Technology: Information Technology Laboratory (2011)
12. Metsch, T., Edmonds, A., Papaspyro, A.: Open Cloud Computing Interface - Core. P-REC Proposed Recommendation, Open Grid Forum (2011) GFD.183 proposed recommendation, http://www.ogf.org/documents/GFD.183.pdf
13. Open Virtualization Format Specification Version 1.1.0. Accessible on DMTF's web-site, http://www.dmtf.org/sites/default/files/standards/documents/DSP0243_1.1.0.pdf
14. Patel, P., Ranabahu, A., Sheth, A.: Service Level Agreement in Cloud Computing. In: Cloud Workshops at OOPSLA 2009 (2009)
15. RESERVOIR Project Web-Site. Project Website, http://62.149.240.97/
16. Topology and Orchestration Specification for Cloud Applications Version 1.0. OASIS Committee Specification Draft 01 (March 08, 2012), http://docs.oasis-open.org/tosca/TOSCA/v1.0/csd01/TOSCA-v1.0-csd01.html
17. WSAG4J - Web Services Agreement for Java. Web site (March 18, 2012), http://packcs-e0.scai.fraunhofer.de/wsag4j

The GreenIT DC-Benchmarking Tool:
From Scientific Theory to Real Life

Ywes Israel and Thomas Leitert

TimeKontor AG
Schoenhauser Allee 10 – 11, 10119 Berlin, Germany
{Ywes.Israel,Thomas.Leitert}@timekontor.de
TimeKontor AG
www.timekontor.de
GreenIT BB
www.greenit-bb.de

Abstract. Energy efficiency is one of the topics in achieving the goal of reducing the CO_2 output in the next years. Data centers (DC) are big polluters. GreenIT DC-Benchmarking is the first neutral benchmarking tool that shows the specific energy and cost saving potential in data centers. By comparison with similar data centers and analysis of best practices, IT managers gain a detailed overview of ways to optimize their systems. The online based comparison tool can be applied to data centers of any type and size. The basic set of data for the GreenIT DC-Benchmarking deviates from a scientific analysis of thirty data centers realized by the Technical University of Berlin. Since April 2010, the stock in the benchmarking tool has grown to 108 data center with more than 79,000 servers.

Keywords: Energy Efficiency & Monitoring, Data Center Benchmarking, Key Performance Indicator, Energy Consumption, Power Usage Effectiveness (PUE).

1 Introduction

Energy Efficiency and Cost Efficiency in Data Centers

On Nov 13th, 2008, the German Council of IT managers decided on the GreenIT goals for the Federal administration [1]. According to these goals, energy consumption in IT should be reduced by 40% – with reference to the year with the highest consumption before 2009 to 2013. Energy consumption of server farms and data center doubled between 2000 and 2008 [2]. Therefore, identifying energy consumption and the energy conservation to the achieved, unified measurement procedures and methods of comparison are needed. As a consequence of the established goals the TU Berlin carried out a design study for energy and resource efficiency. A total of 31 data centers on a total IT area of more than 30,000 m² were subject to a detailed (energy) technology analysis [3]. One of the results showed the average Power Usage Effectiveness (PUE = total facility energy divided by the IT equipment energy) at 1.7 lies considerably below the value that is often cited as the industry wide average (PUE=2). The results developed here for the entire data center system form the basis for additional scrutiny of the topic of IT energy efficiency. Utilizing this data pool, TimeKontor AG, partner in the

J. Huusko et al. (Eds.): E²DC 2012, LNCS 7396, pp. 47–53, 2012.

GreenIT-BB Network[1] Berlin-Brandenburg, developed GreenIT DC-Benchmarking. As of the most current status (April 2012), data from 108 data centers with more than 79.000 servers have already poured in. DC-Benchmarking by the GreenIT-BB Network is the first benchmarking worldwide for the energy and resource efficiency of data centers. It grants decision makers at data centers a quick and reliable overview of potential for savings and optimization. The GreenIT-BB network provides a tool that identifies and exhausts the financial advantages from environmentally sound performance parameters for the hardware and software with which the data center is equipped. At the same time, the user will be in compliance with new legal mandates and targets in the field of energy and environmental protection using this trailblazing method.

In this paper we present the past and future of energy consumption in data centers. Energy costs of data centers are almost not known and taken as an unavoidable topic. Out of the need for information we show the way to collect data with the DC-Benchmarking tool and compare it with the peer group of data center providers.

2   Challenge

2.1   Green in the Grey Zone

Quantifying energy requirements in data centers presents considerable challenges for the operator. They are more than happy to reduce the energy consumption of their data centers, but often don't even know what their energy consumption is due to administrative problems (e.g., questions of responsibility and authority). Additionally, it is increasingly difficult for many to evaluate the efficiency of GreenIT measures. Decision makers increasingly find themselves in a dilemma: on the one hand, complex business processes require increasing use of IT with simultaneously increasing energy costs. On the other hand, they are confronted with the public demand that they reduce their CO_2 emissions. Data centers are also very heterogeneous in size and type. Generally, there aren't any comparable numbers. Finally, until recently there weren't even any reliable models for assessing the overall efficiency of data centers and IT.

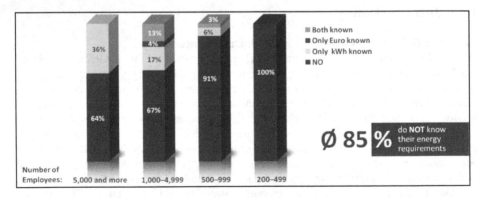

Fig. 1. The bigger the company the less is known about the costs of their data centers [4]

---

[1] GreenIT-BB was founded in 2009 as Public Private Partnership (PPP). The goal is a competence centre for Green IT with rapid and widespread distribution of energy saving ICT.

3   Proposed Solution

3.1   Technical Performance in Direct Comparison

Building on the data from the above mentioned study by the TU Berlin technical benchmarking was developed for data centers. In contrast to business oriented performance comparisons, technical benchmarking analyses the structure and process parameters of data centers. In place of general statements about tendencies toward cost reduction, specialized factual information is in focus here: positioning of individual values, best practices and estimates of potential for approaches to optimizing costs.

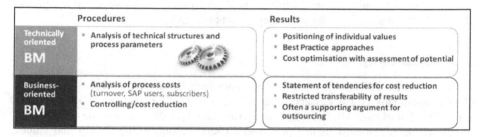

Fig. 2. Comparison of technically oriented and business oriented benchmarking models

An essential element in GreenIT DC-Benchmarking is the realization of the possibility of comparing data centers. To this end, a categorization system was developed. The data centers were assigned to matching peer groups based on the number of servers or CPUs on hand, as well as use area, operational purpose and/ or industry, in order to make a 'comparison of equals' possible.

3.2   Constant Best Performance as a Goal

Along with the comparison with others, you can also subject your own data center to benchmarking at all times and in various states of expansion. The performance of the data center is measurable both permanently and at any time, since all results for 'before/ after' comparisons are archived. Using the benchmark tool, you can easily and plausibly effect potential changes (e.g., new investments or remodels) and new acquisitions.

According to studies, the capacity of data centers grows annually by an average of 17%. This poses enormous challenges for energy efficiency projects: How can savings be plausibly visually during constant growth?

Using the GreenIT computer centre benchmarking, it is possible to neutralize the increase of capacity. The approach is the following:

- depiction of the increase of capacity over the need for electricity in the computer centre's subsections (e.g., number of servers, CPUs, data volume processed and/or stored/archived data volume in the section, UPS, cooling systems);

- neutralization of increased capacity through specific and normed, IT related nominal values (e.g., capacity density per section, energy density per CPU and/or server); and
- option of multiple benchmarking of the same computing centre (before/after comparison).

Beyond this, GreenIT data center benchmarking offers the option of knowledge transfer. Any information on solved specialized problems can be shared with one's own peer group either through communication or by Best Practice Recommendations.

The experiences of the data center benchmarking teams from the studies conducted to date have shown: the greatest GreenIT potential for optimization lies in electricity and cooling requirements for servers, in virtualization and consolidation as well as in optimized use of free cooling. Identified best practices point to sustainable options whereby you can save considerable energy, costs and CO_2.

3.3   Data Security

It is assured that anonymity, neutrality and data security enjoy the highest priority in all processes. This is a necessary precondition for the functioning of GreenIT data center benchmarking. All data generated from the data centers will be strictly and reliably rendered anonymous and processed. There are only some figures and values in the individual basis reports. Additionally, the browser based data center operator data input into the online tool is completed securely through an SSL connection (Secure Sockets Layer). In a Memorandum of Understanding (MoU), the GreenIT-BB Network pledges to treat the data acquired with absolute confidentiality. For their part, the computing centre managers give assurance that they will only use the benchmarking report for internal purposes and not publish it externally.

3.4   Procedure

The benchmarking tool is easy to operate: after free registration, the user is provided with a username and password from the GreenIT DC-Benchmarking team. In the course of acquiring the data by means of an online supported questionnaire, it is possible to save the current status at any time and continue at a later date. Help functions are available for certain aspects of data acquisition.

For identifying performance characteristics, data center benchmarking uses a specially developed set of parameters. The 30 defined individual values, the 'adjusting screws' and 'switching levers', are the factors used for the improvement of resource and energy efficiency in data centers. The investigation also encompasses to collect the number of virtual and physical servers, storage and network components, the quantity of CPUs in use and number of Thin Clients. Additionally other aspects of climate control technology and energy supply are taken into account. Should several data centers belonging to one organization be studied, they can each be named individually – the data will be saved in separate profiles. Under the point 'Centre Management' data can be reviewed and edited. The results are directly accessible from the start page.

In the middle term, determining the load curve through the year is worthwhile. Admittedly, at this time only a few data center operators and IT departments have the corresponding information at their disposal. With optional additional services, GreenIT DC-Benchmarking will support its customers, on request, in the acquisition of measurement data so that they can analyze the distribution of consumption and peak loads. The greater the specificity with which consumption in individual areas can be broken down, the greater the specificity with which potential areas of optimization can be identified and exploited sustainably (e.g., How much power does the UPS use every week?).

4   Results

As a result, the participating data centers will each receive a basic report that provides detailed information about the individual benchmarks in a clear, comprehensible format (e.g., EUE value, power density, energy density, room temperature, cooling equipment). These benchmarks are currently divided into 30 specific values. The individual values are displayed on a scale between Min (worst value) and Max (best value in the peer group) in comparison with the data centers belonging to the same peer group. All values issued are explained in detail and interpreted based on the actual case, and a recommendation is given. If a data center evinces noticeably better performance in one or more benchmark areas in comparison to other data centers in the peer group, these exemplary values are integrated into the reports for other data center benchmarks as best practice recommendations.

The EDPC's energy usage effectiveness (EUE) will be centrally displayed as key performance indicator (KPI).

The GreenIT EDPC radar unites the evaluation of 30 efficiency indicators (W1 – Wn) for the following fields in data processing centers: power density, energy density, energy efficiency, climate control and data management.

Clear, comprehensible graphics with traffic light colors show the status of your own computing centre for each area. If the performance is similar to that of the other data center in your own peer group or better, there may be little need to act. Meeting the maximum demands is, to be sure, a desirable goal that can also be reached in small steps – every single step often brings with it significant cost savings.

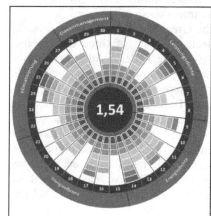

Fig. 3. GreenIT EDPC Radar

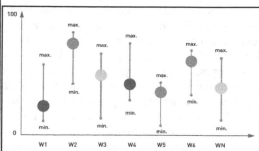

Fig. 4. The evaluation shows the benchmarks (W1 - WN) compared to the peer group. Traffic lights signal the need for optimization.

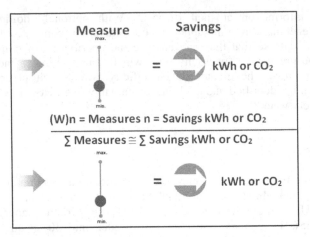

Fig. 5. The simulation of implementing optimization measures forms the basis for a qualified energy efficiency analysis

5   Conclusion and Outlook

"For a ship that doesn't know what harbor it seeks, no wind is favorable."
With this aphorism, the Roman philosopher Seneca pointed over 2,000 years ago just how important a goal oriented focus is in action that will lead to progress. GreenIT DC-Benchmarking presents an offer that is unique worldwide; offering decision makers at data centers a clear course on their way to their goal of improving the energy and resource efficiency of their data centers.

Thereby, the data centers are subjected to technical benchmarking. Operators receive a detailed analysis of the energy and resource efficiency of their data centers with the option of before/after comparisons. According to statements from the Borderstep Institute, there are more than 50,000 data centers only in Germany for which the incomparable potential of GreenIT DC-Benchmarking can offer extraordinary assistance in finding the way to the future. In this sense, GreenIT DC-Benchmarking can serve as your 'lighthouse' in the truest sense of the word.

The Technical DC-Benchmarking Tool from the GreenIT-BB Network impressed the German Federal Administration: it was selected as one of three exceptional lighthouse projects nationwide for Green IT 2010 at the Federal Administration's Green-IT Day on 13th April 2010. The awarding committee commended the effectiveness and future potential of the project for improving IT energy efficiency and recommends the use of the DC-Benchmarking Tools to federal administrative agencies. Here the idea of possible anonymous comparison of federal agencies with other data centers was singled out as exemplary. On an European level this tool can help to standardize the common criteria for collecting sufficient data and comparisons for the development of energy sufficient data centers. It helps to agree with the regulations of the European Commission on Green IT. At the moment a standardization procedure started to officially distribute an Energy Saving Label for the tested data centers.

Acknowledgements. The GreenIT-BB Network and its activities are co-financed with funds of the Joint Agreement for the Improvement of Regional Economic Structures (Federal and State funds).

References

1. The German Federal Ministry of Economics and Technology: Action plan "Germany: Green IT Pioneer", p. 2 (2008), http://www.bmwi.de/English/Redaktion/Pdf/action-plan-green-it-pioneer,property=pdf,bereich=bmwi,sprache=en,rwb=true.pdf
2. Borderstep Insitute: Energyefficient Data Centers – Best-Practice-Examples from Europe, USA and Asia, Berlin, p. 8 (2008), http://www.borderstep.de/pdf/P-Fichter-Clausen-Eimertenbrink-Energy-Efficient_Data_Centres-Best-Practice_Examples_from_Europa_USA_and_Asia-2008.pdf
3. Prof. Dr. rer. Nat. Frank Behrendt, et al.: Konzeptstudie zur Energie- und Ressourceneffizienz im Betrieb von Rechenzentren; TU Berlin, Innovation Centre Energy (IZE) (December 2008) partly financed by TSB Technologiestiftung Berlin, http://www.energie.tu-berlin.de/uploads/media/IZE_Konzeptstudie_Energieeffizienz_in_Rechenzentren.pdf; Main results: The increase in the average server room temperature in conjunction with the increase in the chiller temperature and indirect free cooling helps a lot. With little investment in the building infrastructure greatest savings can be realized. But also for the implementation of pioneering concepts such as combined heat-power-refrigeration (trigeneration) of data centers by district heating are often very good conditions, p. 137
4. Study by Experton Group (2009), http://images.computerwoche.de/images/computerwoche/bdb/493837/C9FE99D05B6E2AB7257C811737B07F55_800x600.jpg (stated June 26, 2009)

GreenSLAs: Supporting Energy-Efficiency through Contracts

Christian Bunse[1], Sonja Klingert[2], and Thomas Schulze[2]

[1] University of Applied Sciences Stralsund
Zur Schwedenschanze 15, 18435 Stralsund, Germany
christian.bunse@fh-stralsund.de
[2] University of Mannheim
A5,6 68161 Mannheim, Germany
{klingert,schulze}@informatik.uni-mannheim.de

Abstract. Outsourcing services from local or personal devices to data centers or the cloud is an ongoing trend in information technology. This trend has led to the expansion of the IT service business and, to a dramatic increase of energy consumption in data centers. One of the objectives of GreenIT is to stop or even reverse this development. Many technical approaches to save energy during the operational phase of a data center are currently being proposed. Unfortunately, a reduction of energy consumption may have a negative impact onto a customer's perceived quality-of-service as denoted in service level agreements (SLAs). Energy aware "GreenSLAs" can help counteracting this dilemma by extending a data center's scope to pursue energy saving measures at runtime. This paper discusses the idea and first empirical results regarding the use of GreenSLAs to balance performance, time, cost, and energy by including semantic information into executable SLAs.

Keywords: Data Centers, Energy, GreenIT, SLA and GreenSLA.

1 Introduction

The clout of ICT on the emergence as well as the solution to eco-sustainability issues (usually referred to as GreenIT) is increasing. In addition to the growth of computing devices in numbers, the popularity of web services and cloud computing is key in this regard. As this leads to an increase not only in energy cost but also in the environmental impact of CO_2 emissions originating in the ICT sphere, energy efficiency is a major goal. Today, research often focuses on (hardware related) aspects such as energy-efficient, low-power hardware or energy harvesting. Most of the - albeit significant - savings, however, are compensated by a growing demand for IT services that are often provided by remote data centers. Since the share of data centers in the carbon footprint is estimated to grow from 14% in 2009 to 18% in 2020, data center management systems need to be improved and enhanced by energy saving strategies [21].

J. Huusko et al. (Eds.): E²DC 2012, LNCS 7396, pp. 54–68, 2012.

Optimizing the energy-consumption of a data center cannot be performed in isolation. Typically data centers must provide their services within the boundaries of a set of quality of service (QoS) characteristics such as performance, availability, security etc, typically specified in service level agreements (SLAs). Until recently, however, energy aspects have hardly ever been included as part of SLA's QoS parameters.

Our solution is the definition and use of specifically adapted SLAs that support service optimization regarding energy consumption. More specifically, we propose the use of resource-aware SLAs, aka "Green Service Level Agreements (GreenSLAs)". GreenSLAs are specified by XML and enriched by semantics, in a way that providers can (re-)arrange their energy optimization activities. In addition, customers have an insight into measurements and a handle to (legally) check service quality. The optimization challenge is that key properties remain within the pre-specified performance boundaries (extended compared to standard, performance-oriented SLA), while at the same time metrics for measuring the energy consumption on a per-service level are introduced and made binding. To achieve this goal we define an SLA validation facility (aka SLA Validator) that checks SLA compliance of provider activities and, in return, triggers (counter-) actions. Thus, GreenSLAs become machine-executable and can be specified/verified in a semi-formal way. The validity of this approach was tested in the context of a small case study which showed that SLAs can be used for configuring energy optimization and that this can be done on a per-service level.

The remainder of the paper is structured as follows. Section two gives an overview about related research. Section three introduces scope and challenges of our research. Section four provides an overview on SLAs in general and discusses the use of semantics for specifying and operating SLAs, aiming at energy aware service optimization. Section five introduces the experimental framework used for validation of our ideas, whereas section six contains a definition of the empirical approach applied and evaluation results. Finally, section eight contains a short summary, some conclusions and presents an outlook for planned future activities.

2   Related Work

Generally, SLAs represent a set of common rules that define the relationship between customer and supplier. As such, they are comparable to legal contracts. More specifically a SLA defines the technical preconditions for executing a job and at the same time determines minimum quality requirements related to this job. As a result of focusing on technical conditions while putting specific attention on performance issues, the relationships between SLA characteristics (technical) and associated energy requirements has often been neglected. Regarding the growing importance of GreenIT the focus either has to shift or be broadened. In the following, we review how existing SLA management approaches can be reused or adapted (i.e., "greened"). In order to do this, we examine energy-saving strategies in computing.

2.1 Enhancing Service Level Agreements

One means for introducing energy related aspects and optimization is to enhance SLAs regarding their expressiveness. Today, SLAs provide a (static) textual specification of key quality properties and legal actions. When it comes to energy related properties, optimizations by the provider may violate quality properties and may lead to customer compensations. Dynamic properties integrated in SLAs can help to specify the strategies, algorithms, etc. so that the data center management becomes more flexible to pursue for instance energy efficiency strategies. Dynamic SLAs are highly adaptable and allow the quick inclusion of new, relevant properties [18, 20] by defining their structure and behavior. This is achieved by defining several ranges of parameters within an SLA [14, 18] and by enabling renegotiation opportunities after agreeing on thus specified meta SLA. In [6] the "dynamics" of an SLA is defined in a different way: It does not relate to the flexibility of an individual SLA tied to an individual job but to an SLA as part of the SLA market. The liquidity in this market can be increased by mapping parameters of private and public SLAs in order to find more matches between supply and demand. [14] shows that there is a trade-off between an increased complexity of SLAs and the need for renegotiation during execution. Technically, some of these approaches make use of multi-agent concepts [18] to distribute observation and replacing "static" QoS parameters by analytical functions.

Although a promising idea, thus enhanced SLAs are not yet used in the context of GreenIT. One of the few examples that integrates energy issues into an SLA framework is [15]: SLAs in cloud computing environments make use of an implementation of the WS-Agreement in order to optimize cloud infrastructure services by adapting resources to SLA requirements. The authors discuss how to integrate a variety of QoS parameters useful for cloud computing into the WS-Agreement, amongst these eco-efficiency parameters like energy consumption, CO_2 emission and compliance with the "European code of conduct".

Another approach that aims at greening the SLA concept are the GreenIT-SLAs developed by Laszewski and Wang [16]. They create "green IT services" and use GreenIT-SLAs in order to monitor the eco-friendliness of a service. This is done via including information about the energy characteristics of a service into the SLA. The paper concentrates on creating energy metrics for green services that can easily be grasped by e.g. relating CO_2 emissions with kilometers driven with a standard middle class car. Thus they focus on monitoring the eco-efficiency of a data center service, however do not steer the energy consumption in a data center.

2.2 Enhancing Workload Management

An overview about a bundle of measures for energy efficient workload management is given in [14]. The authors of [2] and [5] discuss options how to deploy several of these strategies in a data center. They present a plug-in that is located on top of the service management system. The plug-in periodically suggests and executes specifically tailored energy saving techniques (e.g., server consolidation or migration to a federated data center of DVFS). Liu et al. [17] present an architecture for a GreenCloud, also relying on server consolidation through live migration for an online gaming application in a small lab environment whereas [4] focus on the scalability of the energy gains via a virtualized cloud data center.

With the exception of [14] most of the research on energy efficient scheduling and workload management treat SLAs as a performance constraint factor that needs to be complied with in order to fulfill contractual requirements. An example for SLAs being actively used for job scheduling in a supercomputing center is given by [19]. Here new heuristics are suggested to prioritize job scheduling according to SLAs in order to maximize overall system performance - this idea is one foundation for the authors' work on GreenSLAs [13, 14] that is being further developed in the presented paper.

3   Specifying Green Service Level Agreements

SLAs are the technical part of a contract between a provider and its customers specifying key indicators, conditions, contracting partners, etc. As such SLAs are legal documents that should be readable by humans (e.g., managers, lawyers, etc.). To be usable and verifiable at execution-time SLAs also should be specified in a machine-readable way. In this form they serve as an operational basis and allow for just-in-time checks and validations. Even though having been discussed in research for some time, in practice this approach up to now is hardly ever applied. In order to enable data centers to really adopt this technology, research should aim at suggesting solutions that are relatively simple to implement. In this context it is also helpful to create standards so that practioners do not run the risk to rely on a dead-end technology.

As traditional SLAs focus on performance related QoS elements only and do not offer support for customers who intend to optimize the greenness of their business as additional criterion, we developed the concept of GreenSLAs that additionally take eco-efficiency into account. We define GreenSLAs in the following way:

A GreenSLA is a type of SLA between a service provider and its customers that offers an extended scope of energy optimization to the service provider by relaxing traditional performance parameters, by introducing novel energy performance parameters as classifying elements,and by offering incentives to the customers in exchange for a specified degradation of traditional performance metrics.

Thus the GreenSLA modifies the attributes of the underlying service, not its main characteristics. A GreenSLA is always offered alongside a traditional SLA that it compares to.

To provide the content of an SLA in a machine-readable form the use of XML has become a quasi-standard as a language and the use of WS-Agreement a quasi-standard as a deployment framework [3]. It provides an XML schema to specify roles, services, and components that determine the relationship between resource-metrics and SLA parameters, functions, and schedules. It offers enough flexibility to allow the inclusion of energy monitoring [15] and to reference semantic information so that we chose it as preferred framework to design GreenSLAs.

3.1   Eco-efficiency Metrics in SLA

As a first step the energy consumption of a service has to be systematically measured. This requires the definition of (objective) metrics that are agreed upon by provider and customer. In detail eco– or energy-efficiency metrics can be utilized in the following ways:

1. Eco-efficiency metrics can be used to monitor the potential environmental impact of a data center service - which is the topic of [15, 16] Lawrence et al. suggest that monitoring the energy consumption of IT services will per se lead to the optimization of eco-efficiency. In our opinion, monitoring information is neutral: It can be applied in the hope to thereby change the behavior of data center manager and customers into eco-friendliness, but not necessarily.
2. In the next step, eco-efficiency metrics are not only used for monitoring reasons but also as an optimization criterion: This is the direction this paper is taking and an advancement towards GreenSLAs as a fully-fledged steering mechanism. In this case, an eco-efficiency parameter is chosen which is then integrated into an SLA. This is done by enhancing the expressiveness of SLA parameters through behavioral aspects (see section 3.2). Thus the optimization is the second level, based on the monitoring aspect of GreenSLA.
3. Finally, eco-efficiency metrics might be used at the heart of the scheduling mechanism in a data center: As variables of an SLA based scheduling they could be part of a multi-criteria optimization process with both performance and environmental friendliness being optimization goals. In this context the economics of GreenSLAs could come into play by offering new pricing schemes in exchange with performance trade-offs. This will be the next phase of our research.

The nature of metrics in the context of GreenSLAs are manifold: On the one hand GreenSLA contain all metrics of a regular SLA since the nature of the underlying service has not changed. Typically, such metrics describe or support standard monitoring functions. In addition to these metrics, a GreenSLAs will use further criteria to monitor the environmental friendliness of service execution (not to be confounded with the environmental characteristics of the servicing objective). In [15] amongst others the following criteria are suggested as eco-efficiency parameters of a data center service: Energy used for task or resource (in KWh), CO_2 per task or resource (in KG CO_2), yearly average PUE (in a range of 1 - 2.5) or the compliance with the European Data center Code of Conduct.

As it is the goal of GreenSLA to be offered alongside regular SLAs (i.e., as an option for the data center customer to purchase a green service at special conditions), metrics should be simple, closely tied to service execution and directly related to the services' environmental impact. The negative impact of man-made CO_2 emissions is not any longer disputable. Thus, measuring the emission of CO_2 per task would be one simple metric for a GreenSLA that serves as optimization tool. This however, implies the knowledge of the data centers primary energy source. Since such knowledge is typically sparse we decided to use the energy consumption per service as core metric.

3.2   SLA and Behavioral Semantics

When adapting SLAs specified by using XML and WS-Agreement towards the integration of energy related properties, one idea is to define performance and energy metrics as QoS parameters and use them for defining service prices. As suggested by the European research project "Fit4Green"[1] one approach to energy saving is to relax performance metrics and trade-offs against incentive structures. Based on these finding we can go a step further by including behavioral aspects into SLAs. Although unpopular with service providers, we believe that GreenSLAs can not only help to promote energy savings but also help to provide transparent information. In addition, it has to be noted that customers are not longer willing to simply trust a providers' quality promises (i.e., guaranteed bandwidth, etc.). They are desperately asking for legally binding and comprehensive metric definitions, that might also be used for measuring independently from a provider. To achieve these goals we:

1. Implemented an XML-based mechanism for specifying interaction semantics of QoS parameters and pricing options.
2. Suggest ways to balance (energy or monetary) savings among service provider and customer.
3. Investigate where to locate SLA validation: Provider- or customer site. Providers typically have access to important data, but customers have to trust in correct calculation. Vice versa, customers may bear data access problems, while providers have to trust in the customer calculations.
4. Demonstrate the feasibility of monitoring energy consumption on a per-service level.

Integrating semantics into SLAs (in form of XML specs) will increase complexity. Therefore, semantics have to be viewed as an add-on for computers that only needs to be read by experts and machines. Other roles can focus on natural text aspects of the SLA. When using XML we also have to ensure that the specification is well-formed. Since XML data is parsed, a way has to be found to provide behavioral information that is outside the scope of standard parsers. One way to do this is to use XMLs' CDATA construct.

The definition of executable metrics is relatively straightforward. For implementing "simple" metrics/semantics we use the PERL language, since its execution environment is small, efficient, and part of the standard installation of

---

[1] www.fit4green.eu

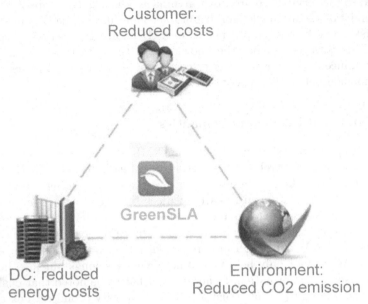

Fig. 1. The Benefit Triangle

most hosts. Disadvantages of this approach are complex and error-prone implementations. To mitigate this problem CDATA sections must therefore follow a common documentation template. Another problem is the consistency of cross-references and dependencies of files and data. If these are out-of-sync calculation problems or errors might occur, leading to unwanted consequences. Therefore, we developed mechanisms to validate dependencies, located in the SLA-Validator (see Fig. 1). Currently we develop an SLA "pre-compiler" that automates this task. The definition of metrics is crucial to foster energy efficiency. Therefore we only define (indirect) metrics in PERL and use a state machine for complex semantics. This is achieved by using the State Chart extensible Markup Language (SCXML) approach[1]. SCXML provides a generic state-machine based execution environment based on Harel statecharts and specifies states and transitions in form of XML tags. In the context of this paper we realized a draft implementation of the SCXML interpretation algorithm [1]. Due to the nature of XML of being extensible, CDATA sections and SCXML sections can be "easily" integrated into WSDL based specifications of Service Level Agreements. The result is an "executable" SLA that provides semantic regarding the collection and use of energy data.

4   Framework

In general energy (measured in Joule) is a function of voltage and ampere over time. Thus, the energy consumption of a service or application cannot, in contrast to properties such as time be directly measured. Unfortunately, standard energy-measurement devices cannot be used to measure the energy consumption of software since such devices provide rough estimations for complete devices that are prone to wideband noise. Other strategies such as ACPI (Advanced Configuration and Power Interface) [12] requires that operating system has exclusive control of all aspects of power management and device configuration. But, energy values are means that cover time periods of one minute or more. Thus, for the goals of this study ACPI does not provide the required precision. In addition most of such devices are not designed for the low voltages and currents that are used in computing systems. Thus, unfortunately, the use of low-budget measurement units is not feasible for this research.

Therefore, for this study we decided to follow an alternative path to energy measurement. Energy consumption can be measured via examining voltage drops, at a sense resistor, of a system for the duration of a service or application execution. Energy can then be calculated, following Ohm's and Kirchhoff's law, by calculating the integral of the curve defined by the data. Using resistors for measurement purposes requires the use of specifically designed sense resistors that have a low error limit.

This method to measure the energy consumption on CPU level of an IT service is quite cumbersome and for the practice not yet feasible - for lab experiments however, it has proven to give stable results and a good first assessment. In real environments the approach presented in [14] is easier to carry through: Certain energy strategies that are known to result in specific energy savings are grouped together in energy saving categories.

4.1 Energy Measurement in Data Centers

Today data centers (i.e., service providers) use techniques such as virtualization to centralize administrative tasks while improving scalability, energy consumption and workload. In practice several virtual machines (each probable executing a different application and/or service) are executed on one (physical) host. Even if energy-consumption data for a machine and/or environment can be obtained it is not directly mapped to a service or application. Therefore mechanisms have to be found to distribute energy data according to the concrete share of a virtual device. This is a very complex task as neither the number of virtual machines per physical server remains constant over time, nor there is a simple way to determine which virtual machine (provided we know its whereabouts and longevity) caused which percentage of energy used by the physical host.

4.2 Energy Optimization Strategies

Dynamically optimizing the energy consumption of computing systems depends on energy-efficient hardware and software in combination with strategy-based optimization. As such one can improve the software being executed [3, 7, 8, 11] (client side) and the way service requests are handled and organized (provider side)[2]. As discussed in [11] there are quite a couple of available strategies (e.g., virtualization or energy-aware workload (re)-allocation) In the context of this paper (i.e., within the performed cases study) we made use of standard energy saving strategies (e.g., I/O data compression and dynamic voltage and frequency scaling) that are provided by the operating system and hardware platform. These were supported by software optimization strategies that are based on the use of resource allocation strategies [7, 10] that dynamically choose the "best" resource for a given task (e.g., exchanging CPU power with memory, etc.).

4.3   SLA-Based Control

GreenSLAs can help the data center operating in the classic quality triangle so that service provision and execution is optimal for all involved actors [16]:

1. For the data center in terms of reduced energy cost (i.e., savings up to 50% are possible [2]).
2. For customers of an energy-optimized data center customer in terms of a reduced price (if she accepts reduced QoS).
3. For the natural environment in terms of reduced CO_2 emissions.

This can be reached by relaxing the parameters of the GreenSLA in comparison with the regular SLA with regard to e.g. performance or accessibility metrics in order to increase the data center's scope for energy saving measures. Thus, optimization (of energy) has to be controlled to ensure navigation within the triangle. In the context of this paper we used an adapted version of the Energy Management Component (EMC) introduced in [8]. At its core the EMC contains several energy saving strategies and makes them controllable following a strategy pattern approach. In addition the EMC uses a cost model to "know" the cost and impact of service requests for selecting the most suitable one. Thus, the cost model "decides" if and which optimization strategy is used guided by the actual SLA.

5   Case Study

In order to evaluate the ideas and principles underlying GreenSLAs we defined and conducted an empirical study that examined SLA-based energy management in the context of web-services and mobile clients. The goal of the study is to provide first insights and trends. In the future the study approach will be migrated to a real data centers in order to obtain realistic data.

5.1   Experimental Set-Up

The study is used to evaluate the use of GreenSLAs in the context of webservices. These services are hosted by a service provider (i.e., "model data-center") represented by a barebone PC. The platform provides interfaces to measure energy consumption of system components. In addition the hosts' management software was adapted [11] to enable energy saving strategies. Energy data is collected by a separate unit in order to reduce measurement overheads and increase data quality. A server, providing JSON and REST based (web-) services is running on this machine. SLA validation is located on a separate host. The location of the "SLA Validator" can be freely chosen. It collects energy data as well as other provider- or customer data and identifies SLA violations regarding energy, time, and performance. The service provider is informed about identified violations to enable counteraction. In addition all data is logged separately for later analysis'. Clients that make use of the services. In order to generate load and since we are also interested in reducing the energy consumption of such devices [11] we used smart phones as client platforms. In practice we used a mixture of PC-based emulations and real devices.

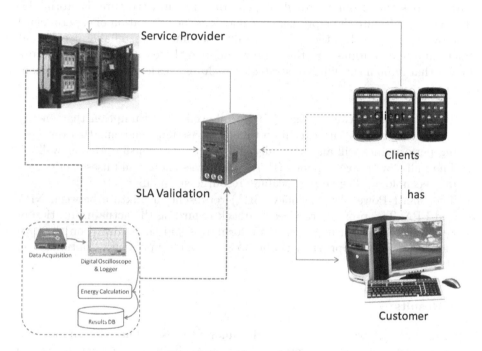

Fig. 2. Experimental Setup

The study focus was to examine GreenSLAs regarding balancing time, cost and energy consumption. As such optimization approaches and policies were not in the focus of our research. However, recent results [8, 9] indicate that the optimization overhead is small and will not exceed obtained savings.

5.2 Experimental Design

We claim that GreenSLAs or more specifically: SLAs that include behavior specifications as well as energy metrics, are a suitable means for organizing and controlling the optimization of energy and quality properties. To evaluate this idea we defined three different SLAs (i.e., to simulate different customers) that use the aforementioned technology, each oriented towards a specific goal. In detail we created: (A), a standard SLA (Full Power) which did not address energy consumption at all but prioritizes performance and time; (B), a variant (i.e., Relaxed SLA) that specifies key indicators not within tight boundaries but "relaxes" these by 30%; in addition, energy became a key indicator.And (C), an energy-aware SLA (GreenJob) that uses tight energy ranges as a key indicator.

5.3   Experimental Runs

The execution/evaluation of different SLAs within one infrastructure always bears the risk that results strongly depend on this infrastructure. Factorial designs help to mitigate these problems by allowing the estimation of experimental error by replication. In other words, results become more reliable if collected under varying conditions. We therefore we defined three different infrastructure policies that implement different strategies/technologies for energy optimization. In detail:

1. The Non-Power-Aware policy (NPA) followed the assumption that energy strongly correlates with execution time. The assumption being that optimizing performance will automatically improve energy consumption as well.
2. The Full-Power-Aware policy (FPA) prioritizes energy and uses energy saving technologies like voltage-scaling, resource-substituion, etc.
3. The Smart-Power-Aware policy (SPA) represents a mixture between NPA and FPA. The provider receives feedback regarding the actual utilization of key indicators regarding energy, performance and time. Based on the provided feedback the provider is able to select and apply energy optimization strategies.

5.4   Results

Experimental data was collected over the different runs and normalized for every run. Data was collected for every service request. Energy measurement (see 1) communicates with SLA validation and service provider. These are creating signals that indicate when to start or stop measurement. SLA violations and quality properties were collected and calculated for every run. A violation is recorded when the measured value is outside the specified range or above a threshold. In addition, we calculated the total consumed energy (in KWh) at the provider site. Furthermore we calculated an average value for the energy consumption per service request (in Joule). Table 1 contains the results.

Results indicate that a typical service requires 5.8J at the provider site, which sums up to 8.56KWh for executing the complete sequence of requests. Energy consumption can be optimized to a minimum of 1.14KWh or 0.7J per request when energy optimization is key priority of the infrastructure. However, not surprisingly this leads to a quite high number of SLA violations regarding performance and time (20.3%). Using smart or balanced optimization helps to reduce

Table 1. Experimental Results

Run	SLA								
	Full Power			Relaxed			GreenJob		
	Energy	Violations		Energy	Violations		Energy	Violations	
	Total	QoS	Energy	Total	QoS	Energy	Total	QoS	Energy
1 (NPA)	8.56 KWh	0.05%	---	8.56 KWh	0.05%	5.43%	8.56 KWh	0.05%	9.04%
2 (FPA)	1.14 KWh	20.3%	---	1.14 KWh	20.3%	1.23%	1.14 KWh	20.3%	0.05%
3 (SPA)	6.51 KWh	8.96%	---	2.98 KWh	5.74%	2.33%	1.48 KWh	2.21%	0.57%

energy consumption to 6.51 KWh and 4.4J per service request while keeping the number of SLA violations quite low (8.96% in case of the "Full Power" SLA).

When relaxing SLA requirements towards GreenSLAs) we can obtain an average reduction to 2.98KWh or 2J per Job while keeping SLA violations regarding the other factors at 5.47%. These findings are supported by the results regarding the "Green Job" SLA. Since the key factors are even more relaxed optimization can reach an energy consumption of 1.48KWh or 1J in average while other SLA violations are around 2.21. In addition, the latter two SLAs also defined energy consumption levels. Smart optimization was able to obtain low energy-related SLA violation rates of 2.33% and 0.57%.

5.5 Threats to Validity

The results of the study are limited and cannot be easily generalized or transferred to other domains. In this regard the following threats were identified:

- Energy consumption is a difficult concept to measure. The used approach, although feasible in a lab setting, might be difficult to use in the context of larger data centers. Here approaches that make use of existing energy measurement interfaces might be more suitable.
- Possibly the relation between energy data and the executed service is imprecise. To minimize this threat, we replicated the execution of request sequences and normalized results.
- The materials (platforms, software, etc.) may not be representative in terms of size and complexity. However, experiments in a university context do not allow the use of realistic systems for reasons such as cost, availability, etc. Nevertheless, the authors view this study as exploratory and view its results as indicators that allow further research.

6 Summary and Conclusions

In this paper we presented an approach for using SLA in the context of energy optimization. We addressed the problem of including semantic information regarding metrics and behavior into text-based SLA specifications and presented first steps how to collect energy-data on a per service request basis. We discussed requirements for metrics to be used for GreenSLAs and chose a simple metric useful for our first approximation within a lab situation. Finally we evaluated our findings in the context of a feasibility study and thus showed that smart energy optimization using GreenSLAs for configuration and control can obtain significant savings (between 1.4J and 4.8J per service request, depending on SLA type) while keeping the number of SLA violation low (QoS: 2.21%-8.96%, Energy 0.57%-2.33%).

The study serves as a proof on concept that, in principle, SLAs can be used to control energy optimization activities of a service provider. In addition to simply saving energy in a technically feasible way, smart approaches have to be aware of other context requirements such as those defined by SLAs (i.e. the economic forces of markets). Due to side-effects, the technologically optimal energy solution is in most of the cases not economically viable. Smart optimization therefore has to balance performance, time, cost, and energy consumption using market forces and incentives. As a prerequisite for this approach we have shown that it is possible to include semantic information into an SLA and by making SLAs thus "executable" to shift the energy-performance balance more into the direction of saving energy. However, we need more realistic data to investigate the practical applicability of our findings.

One of the studies major threats was the generalization of results (i.e., real-life data from an actual data center is needed) from the data and scalability point of view. Currently we are in discussion with the universities' local data centers. As an intermediate step we are preparing a test-bed that makes use of the CloudSim environment since this is a "cheap" alternative in comparison to "real" runs. We are extending the framework regarding energy aware simulations and the ability to account SLA violations. The simulated data center will then consist of more than 100 heterogeneous physical nodes. In parallel, we are planning to adapt commercial products like the Rackwise DCM, VMWare or the Tivoli Framework from IBM regarding the ideas of our approach.

Another direction our next research phase is taking is to include the economics of SLA markets into the approach.This refers to the second issue in the scope of research we are targeting (see section 3). In the presented work we merely touched upon this question; however it will be necessary to further explore the trade-off between energy savings and performance in order to offer realistic incentives of price and performance to customers and to show under which conditions GreenSLA are acceptable and will become an economic as well as environmental success.

Acknowledgments. This research has been partly (Sonja Klingert and Thomas Schulze) carried out within the European Project FIT4Green (FP7-ICT-2009-4). Details on the project, its goals and results can be found at: http://www.fit4green.eu.

References

1. Barnett, J., Akolkar, R., Auburn R.J., Bodell, M., Burnett, D.C., Carter, J., Mc-Glashan, S., Lager, T., Helbing, M., Hosn, R., Raman, T.V., Reifenrath, K.: W3C Working Draft (2010), http://www.w3.org/TR/2010/WD-scxml-20101216/
2. Basmadjian, R., Bunse, C., Georgiadou, V., Giuliani, G., Klingert, S., Lovasz, G., Majanen, M.: FIT4Green - Energy aware ICT Optimization Policies. In: Proceedings of the COST Action IC0804 on Energy Efficiency in Large Scale Distributed Systems - 1st Year (2010)
3. Battré, D., Wieder, P., Ziegler, W.: WS-Agreement Specification Version 1.0 Exp. Document Open Grid Forum (2010)
4. Beloglazov, A., Buyya, R., Lee, Y.C., Zomaya, A.Z.: A Taxonomy and Survey of Energy-Efficient Data Centers and Cloud Computing Systems. Advances in Computers 82 (2011)
5. Berl, A., Gelenbe, E., Di Girolamo, M., Giuliani, G., De Meer, H., Dang, M.-D., Pentikousis, K.: Energy-Efficient Cloud Computing. The Computer Journal 53(7) (September 2010)
6. Breskovic, I., Maurer, M., Emeakaroha, V.C., Brandic, I.: Towards Autonomic Market Management in Cloud Computing Infrastructures. In: CLOSER 2011 (2011)
7. Bunse, C., Höpfner, H.: Resource substitution with components - Optimizing Energy Consumption. In: Proc. of the 3rd ICSOFT, Setubal, Portugal, pp. 28–35. INSTICC Press (2008)
8. Bunse, C., Höpfner, H.: Energieeffiziente Software-Systeme. In: Halang, W.A., Holleczek, P. (eds.) Eingebettete Systeme — Proc. of the Real-time 2010 Workshop (Echtzeit 2010), Boppard. Informatik aktuell, November 18-19. Springer (2010)
9. Bunse, C., Höpfner, H.: Analyse des Zusammenhangs zwischen Energiebedarf, Dienstgüte und Performanz bei der Ressourcensubstitution in Software-Systemen. In: Halang, W.A., Holleczek, P. (eds.) Eingebettete Systeme — Proc. of the Real-time 2011 Workshop (Echtzeit 2011), Boppard. Informatik aktuell. Springer, Heidelberg (2011)
10. Bunse, C., Höpfner, H.: Energy Awareness Needs a Rethinking in Software Development. In: Cuaresma, M.J. E., Shishkov, B., Cordeiro, J. (eds.) ICSOFT 2011 - Proceedings of the 6th International Conference on Software and Data Technologies, Seville, Spain, July 18-21, vol. 2 (2011)
11. Buyya, R., Ranjan, R., Calheiros, R.N.: Modeling and simulation of scalable cloud computing environments and the CloudSim toolkit: Challenges and opportunities. In: Proceedings of the 7th High Performance Computing and Simulation Conference (HPCS 2009). IEEE Press, USA (2009)
12. HP Corp., Intel Corp., Microsoft Corp., Phoenix technologies Ltd and Toshiba Corp.: Advanced Configuration and Power Interface Specification. Revision 4.0.a (April 2010)
13. Klingert, S., Bunse, C.: GreenSLAs for Energy Efficient Scheduling. In: Proceedings of the COST Action IC0804 on Energy Efficiency in Large Scale Distributed Systems (2011)

14. Klingert, S., Schulze, T., Bunse, C.: GreenSLAs for the Energy-efficient Management of Data centers. In: Second International Conference on Energy-efficient Computing and Networking (E-Energy 2011), New York (2011)
15. Lawrence, A., Djemame, K., Wäldrich, O., Ziegler, W., Zsigri, C.: Using Service Level Agreements for Optimising Cloud Infrastructure Services. In: Cezon, M., Wolfsthal, Y. (eds.) ServiceWave 2010 Workshops. LNCS, vol. 6569, pp. 38–49. Springer, Heidelberg (2011)
16. von Laszewski, G., Wang, L.: GreenIT Service Level Agreements. In: Gridworkshop Collocated with IEEE-ACM GRID 2009 Conference, Canada (2009)
17. Liu, L., Wang, H., Liu, X., Jin, X., He, W., Wang, Q., Chen, Y.: GreenCloud: A New Architecture for Green Data Center. In: The 6th International Conference on Autonomic Computing and Communications, Barcelona, Spain (June 16, 2009)
18. Ouelhadj, D., Garibaldi, J.M., MacLaren, J., Sakellariou, R., Krishnakumar, K.T.: A Multi-agent Infrastructure and a Service Level Agreement Negotiation Protocol for Robust Scheduling in Grid Computing. In: Sloot, P.M.A., Hoekstra, A.G., Priol, T., Reinefeld, A., Bubak, M. (eds.) EGC 2005. LNCS, vol. 3470, pp. 651–660. Springer, Heidelberg (2005)
19. Sakellarriou, R., Yarmolenko, V.: Job Scheduling on the Grid: Towards SLA-Based Scheduling. In: Grandinetti, L. (ed.) High Performance Comp. and Grids in Action. Adv. in Parallel Comp., vol. 16 (2009)
20. Spillner, J., Schill, A.: Dynamic SLA Template Adjustments Based on Service Property Monitoring. In: 2009 IEEE International Conference on Cloud Computing, pp. 183–189 (2009)
21. Webb, M., et al.: SMART 2020: Enabling the low carbon economy in the information age. The Climate Group London (2008),
http://www.ecoc2008.org/documents/SYMPTu_Webb.pdf

Power-Aware Resource Allocation
for CPU- and Memory-Intense Internet Services

Vlasia Anagnostopoulou[1], Susmit Biswas[1], Heba Saadeldeen[1],
Ricardo Bianchini[2], Tao Yang[1], Diana Franklin[1], and Frederic T. Chong[1]

[1] Department of Computer Science, University of California, Santa Barbara
{vlasia,susmit,heba,tyang,franklin,chong}@cs.ucsb.edu
[2] Department of Computer Science, Rutgers University
ricardob@cs.rutgers.edu

Abstract. Internet service providers face the daunting task of maintaining guaranteed latency requirements while reducing power requirements. In this work, we focus on a class of services with very high cpu and memory demands, best represented by internet search. These services provide strict latency guarantees defined in Service-Level Agreements, yet the clusters need to be flexible to different optimizations, i.e. to minimize power consumption or to maximize resource usage. Unfortunately, standard cluster algorithms, such as resource allocation, are oblivious of the SLA allocations, while power management is typically only driven by cpu demand. We propose a *power-aware resource allocation* algorithm for the cpu and the memory which is driven by SLA and allows for various dynamic cluster configurations, from energy-optimal to resource-usage-optimal. Using trace-based simulation of two service models, we show that up to 24% energy can be preserved compared to the state-of-art scheme, or maximum memory utility can be achieved with 20% savings.

Keywords: Internet-services, Datacenter-clusters, Power management, Resource allocation, Request-distribution, Caching.

1 Introduction

The cpu- and memory-intense service class includes services with increasing popularity, such as internet-search, social networks and online gaming applications (identified by Kozyrakis et al. in [1] and Meisner et al. in [2]). Like all internet services, the quality of these services is defined in terms of the service latency, and for this reason, service providers usually provide with latency guarantees defined in *Service-Level Aggreements (SLAs)*. From an infrastructure's perspective, it is critical for the host cluster to provide with adequate resources for the service to achieve its SLA (via resource allocation algorithms). What is more, the cluster requires software to manage its intense energy consumption (via power management), and software to manage the service's performance (i.e. the latency), typically a distributed request distribution algorithm.

Unfortunately, the design and scope of resource allocation algorithms does not address adequately the challenges of datacenter clusters. First of all, they have

J. Huusko et al. (Eds.): E²DC 2012, LNCS 7396, pp. 69–80, 2012.
© Springer-Verlag Berlin Heidelberg 2012

been traditionally designed to run at the system-level; without awareness of the service's SLA, they may assign allocations which are unable to satisfy the SLA. Secondly, resource allocation algorithms are tuned to a fixed objective, e.g. to maximize resource utilization. However, unlike stand-alone or small distributed systems, internet-clusters need to adjust to various operational scenarios. For example, the cluster may need to host a second service after another datacenter experiences a sudden or a maintenance-related downtime, or the cluster may need to expand to the servers of another cluster when a large spike appears in the service's load, such as in a Slash-dot effect. In either case, the cluster will have to dynamically adjust its objective, i.e. from optimizing energy savings, to guaranteeing minimum levels of performance to each of the services.

Power management algorithms typically consolidate the load dynamically into a subset of servers, such that a target SLA is achieved ([3], [4], [5], [6], [7]). Although, compared to resource allocation algorithms, these algorithms do implement a notion of SLA, they too are inadequate for managing clusters running cpu- and memory-intense applications. A major issue is that they are commonly driven by CPU demand only, without taking into account the demand for the rest of the resources. Yet, being oblivious of the memory demand, they may result in configurations which fail to satisfy the application's memory demand. Lastly, by operating at the server-level, power management algorithms leave unexploited the potential for deeper power savings that resource-level management can only achieve. From the above, we motivate ourselves to codesign resource allocation and power management into a single *power-aware resource allocation algorithm*, such that to address datacenter cluster challenges efficiently.

Request distribution helps maximize the service's latency. The main function of this algorithm is to eliminate long latencies via load-balancing, and to leverage the reoccurence of popular requests via the use of a global caching scheme. Despite its integrity in the management of datacenter clusters, this algorithm carries a rather obsolete design created for web-clusters ([8], [9], and [4]), which does not "match" with the design elements of datacenter cluster algorithms that we mentioned above. In particular, request distribution typically assumes a fixed set of serving servers. Yet, the power and resource management algorithms adjust the serving set of servers dynamically. Although this algorithm is not directly related to resource and power management, we feel that it is important to adjust its design such that it would be possible to work with the power-aware resource allocation on an actual deployment.

1.1   Problem Definition

Our target system consists of a datacenter cluster which hosts one, or more, cpu- and memory-intense applications. The latency of the applications is restricted by SLAs. A server can be active, turned off, or in a low-power state. The cluster must be dynamically configured to optimize one of the following objectives: energy-efficiency or memory utilization, The cluster must run a number of management algorithms at its middleware: resource-allocation, power management and request distribution with global caching. In our design, we substitute resource-allocation and power management with a single power-aware resource allocation algorithm.

Problem: 1) Dynamic, periodic SLA-based cluster configuration at the granularity of cpu and memory, such that SLA level latency is achieved, while energy consumption is minimized, or memory utilization is maximized. 2) At regular operation, schedule requests such that they are aware of the current cluster configuration.

1.2   Contributions

Our contributions can be summarized as: (1) We codesign an efficient and configurable dynamic resource and power management solution targeting datacenter clusters; (2) using trace-drive simulation from two cpu and memory- intense service traces, we show that up to 24% more energy can be saved, compared to memory-oblivious power management (42% savings compared to no power management); (3) we also show that our scheme can maximize the utility of memory with up to 20% energy savings (34% to no power management), or enable the sharing of multiple applications to achieve particular SLAs; and (4) we are the first to our knowledge to consider all layers of cluster management during the design of our management algorithm, by adjusting the design of the request distribution algorithm as well.

The organization of our paper is as follows: in Section 2 we provide with the background of the cluster management algorithms and present the related work to ours, in Section 3 we provide with the details of our design, in Section 4 we discuss the details of our simulation infrastructure, in Section 5 we present our experiments, results and some discussion, while in Section 6 we conclude the paper.

2   Background and Related Work

Power management has been explored by various researchers ([3], [5], [10], [4], [11], [6], [7]). Elnozahy et al. in [3] proposed the base power management algorithm where servers are dynamically allocated based on the service load and the rest are turned off. The work of Rajamani et al. in [4] investigated combined power-performance management, by integrating request distribution with power management. The common issue among these solutions is that they estimate the cluster configuration based only the cpu demand of the application, ignoring its memory demand. Although in our work we follow the rough concept of Rajamani et al. and combine performance-power management, our scheme is unique from all other solutions in that it additionally takes memory demand into account, it enables the hosting of multiple applications and it can adjust the objective of its configuration dynamically.

Low-power states, which offer fast transition latencies (e.g. in the order of msecs) while consuming a small fraction of power, have been proposed by Meisner et al. in [12], Agarwal et al. in [13], and Anagnostopoulou et al. in [14]). However, from these states, only Anagnostopoulou et al. enable the memory to be powered on while the server is in low-power state, a requirement of our algorithm. Their state is called *barely-alive.*

Standard request distribution algorithms prioritize avoiding disk accesses as long as the requests do not overwhelm the server, in favor of remote memory accesses. The algorithm requires a *directory* structure, which is used to hold the mappings between servers and their cached requests, such that to enable remote memory caching. The remote-accessing request distribution algorithm was first proposed by Pai et al. in [8], and extended to a distributed version by Carrera et al in [9]. In this work, we use as our base request distribution algorithm the one that is described in [9], and adjust for barely-alive servers.

Zhou et al. in [15] proposed a hardware and software mechanism for memory allocation based on optimizing the memory performance. The underlying mechanism of their scheme is Mattson't stack algorithm described in [16]. The ideas of maximizing memory utilization using performance hints by the hit-counters described in Mattson't work are also explored by Qureshi et al. in [17] among others. In this work, we extend the caching layer of the request distribution algorithm to perform SLA-based memory allocation, yet we use the same mechanism for performance monitoring such as Zhou and Mattson.

3   Middleware

The overview of our system and algorithms has been described in Section 1, at the Problem definition paragraph. Here we provide with the details of our algorithms, and some aspects which are particularly important in the implementation of the algorithms.

3.1   Basic Power-Aware Resource Allocation

Hard and Soft SLAs. One important aspect of the power-aware resource allocation algorithm is the target performance. We define two levels of SLAs, to represent the different configuration objectives, i.e. maximization of the energy savings or the resource utilization. The *hard SLA* is the minimum acceptable level of performance for the service, while the *soft SLA* is the maximum level of performance achieved with management. In other words, the hard SLA represents the conservative performance level, where the energy savings are maximized, while the soft SLA represents the loose level, where the resource utilization is maximized.

SLA/Cluster Configuration. Configuring the cluster implies transitioning each server into any of three types of states: active, barely-alive and off. *Active* servers contribute both their cpu and memory capacity, while consuming power proportional to the load. Servers in *barely-alive* only contribute their memory capacity, while consuming a low power consumption. Servers which are *turned-off* do not contribute any capacity but consume no power. In terms of allocations, the hard SLA is achieved by consolidating the load into the minimum number of servers, which satisfies both cpu and memory demands (*active* servers). The soft SLA is achieved by using the minimum number of servers to meet the cpu demand only, and the rest of the servers is transitioned to *barely-alive* state, such that maximum memory is made available. *Both of these targets are defined in terms of the baseline performance, i.e. the service response time when no management is applied.* The formulas which calculate the required number of servers such to guarantee the cpu and memory demands are given by the equations below.

$$N_{active} = Load/Server\text{-}CPU\text{-}capacity \qquad (1)$$

$$N_{active} + N_{barely-alive} = Mem\text{-}demand/Server\text{-}Mem\text{-}capacity \qquad (2)$$

The server cpu capacity is simply a percentage of the maximum server capacity. This is used as a switch to control the aggressiveness of power management. For example, using an effective server capacity of 80%, the algorithm will transition more servers compared to an effective capacity of 60%. We use as a tuning parameter for the aggressiveness of energy savings in our experimentation.

The power-aware resource allocation algorithm configures the cluster for a target SLA (hard or soft). In general, configuring the cluster consists of setting both the server states and the memory allocations of the servers. However, in its basic form, the algorithm only adjusts the states of the servers, allocating all of the servers' available resource capacities. Below we present the pseudo-code of the basic algorithm. N_{active} and $N_{barely-alive}$ can be calculated using the Equations (1) and (2).

```
Data:
N: num of servers in cluster

Configure for max energy savings:
 activate N_active servers
 if N_barely-alive > N_active then
      transition N_barely-alive - N_active servers to barely-alive
      turn N - N_barely-alive + N_active servers off
 else
      turn N - N_active servers off

Configure for max memory utilization:
 activate N_active servers
 transition N - N_active servers to barely-alive
```

In order to illustrate this formulas, assume a hypothetical cluster featuring five servers, each with 1GB memory capacity and cpu capacity of 1000 connections. Assume also that the service at one point has a load of 3000 connections, and requires 4GB of memory allocation, in order to achieve its SLA latency. The minimum number of servers to service the load is 3, while the minimum number of servers to satisfy the memory allocation is 4. In the energy-efficiency oriented configuration, the algorithm would activate 3 servers, transition 1 to barely-alive and turn 1 server off. In the maximal memory utilization case, the algorithm would activate 3 servers and transition 2 to barely-alive, increasing the effective memory of the cluster by 1GB.

3.2   Full Power-Aware Resource Allocation

SLA/Memory Allocation. Machine-level allocation introduces several bottlenecks, such as not being able to share the memory with more than one applications and potentially waste memory power when more memory than the one required is kept active. To tackle this problem, we utilize the stack-based memory-performance monitoring technique by Zhou et al in [15], which enables proportioning the memory at a fine granularity (see Section 2). Because this technique monitors hits (and subsequently hit-rates) with size, we add a mapping between SLAs and hit-rates. To illustrate this extra mapping level, let us use an example from our experiments: SLA level #1 requires 13GB of memory allocation. This allocation corresponds to a hit-rate of 33%. The SLA level is input to the power-aware allocation algorithm, yet at the caching level, the respective hit-rate is used.

SLA/Memory Sharing. When multiple services share the cluster memory, we need to ensure a fair way to split the memory among the services. We utilize the memory-performance monitoring mechanism, but we maintain performance stacks for each service. To ensure a fair way of proportioning memory when the memory is not enough to satisfy all target allocations, we device an optimization problem, which maximizes an aggregate performance metric. In particular, we solve a linear optimization problem, where the sum of the distances between the actual performance and SLA for each of the applications is minimized, subject to the cluster memory capacity. We assume uniform memory allocations among the active servers for each service. Below, we present the exact algorithm.

```
Data:
  N: number of services
  M: global memory capacity
  alloc_i: memory allocation of service i
  perf_i: performance of service i
  l: list of services

Initialization:
  alloc_i = 0, for i = 1,.., N
  l = add all services

Main loop:
  while (∑_{i=1}^{N} alloc_i < M && l! = empty)
      find service s in l with min{SLA - perf}
      alloc_s+ = cache-block
      perf' = perf estimate of s after allocation
      if (perf' >= SLA) then
          remove service s from l
```

The algorithm also distinguishes between applications having a priority of 100% or 0. In particular, if an application has priority 100%, then it can allocate up to all the rest of the memory, after the minimum level of hard SLA has been met for each of the rest of the applications. In this case, we would run the above algorithm for a minimum level of SLA, and then let the high priority application claim as much from the rest of the memory as it requires.

Final Algorithm. The user inputs a high level objective, i.e. maximize savings or resource utilization, and tentatively a set of priorities for each of the applications. The algorithm first runs the basic portion of the algorithm which estimates the states of the servers based on the user-level objective. Depending on the setting, the algorithm may also invoke the memory managing portion of the algorithm which allocates memory at a fine-franularity. If more than one applications are sharing the cluster, then the algorithm must run the memory sharing algorithm, taking into account the set of priorities.

3.3   Adjusted Request Distribution

The request distribution algorithm needs to be adjusted in order to include servers in a barely-alive state. Note however that the order of the original algorithm will have to be maintained, i.e. remote memory accesses are prioritized so long as no overload is incurred. Therefore, we suggest that the algorithm first checks for a request in the remote memory of active servers, and only if the request is not found there, it checks in the remote memory of the barely-alive servers. Because a barely-alive server cannot service requests on its own, the current server (the initial server from Round-robin) needs to be checked for an overload. If an overload is not an issue, then the current server accesses passively (i.e. without updating the cache or the hit information), remotely the memory of the barely-alive server where the request was found. Otherwise, the algorithm resumes as originally designed.

4   Methodology

4.1   Simulator

The application traces are input to the simulator, which distributes and calculates the impact of each request on the cluster. The application traces consist of tuples (*object-id, object-size, timestamp*), where the timestamp indicates the arrival time of the request. The output of the simulator is a set of performance and power statistics, namely the current *power*, the *cluster load*, the *service latency*, and the *memory hit-rate*. The requests are distributed to the servers based on the request distribution algorithm.

On each request, the simulator updates the performance and power statistics. The performance is calculated based on the latency characteristics of actual hardware components, and the size of the request. Because of lack of space, we have to omit presenting here the latency parameters. The power is calculated using the power parameters shown in Table 1, and a linear power model where the power is proportional to the load (such as in [18]). Additional metrics being updated include the load of the serving server, which is incremented with the time frame of the request. Also, the LRU stack of the serving server is updated, in case the access is a hit, then the hit counter corresponding to the position of the stack where the request was found is incremented.

Table 1. Server power consumption by component

Component	Active	BA
Core i7 (Xeon 5500)	94-260W	18W (2)
Atom (D500)		
1 Gbit/sec NI	5W	5W
2 Hitachi Deskstar 7K-1000	24W	4W
500MB laptop disk		
DRAM	12W (4GB)	12W (4GB)
Fans	50W (5)	10W (1)
Small embedded CPU		1W
Power supply loss	37-53W	10W
	(20%-15%)	(20%)
Total	222-404W	60W

4.2 Service Traces

We simulate a "snippet" generator for internet-search, that services search queries by returning a query-dependent summary of the top-10 search results. We obtained a 7-day trace representing a fraction of the query traffic directed to a popular search engine (Ask.com) measured in query rate. The volume of queries follows the traditional pattern of peaks during the day and troughs during the night. Weekend traffic follows a similar pattern but with lower traffic. In order to generate a complete workload, we also analyze publicly available traces that contain all submitted queries (36.39 Million) to AOL over a duration of 3 months in 2006. The distribution of object requests follows a Zipfian distribution. We ran a sample of AOL queries against Ask.com, downloaded the content pointed to by the URLs listed in the returned results, and computed the content size. We found a median size of 6 Kbytes following a Gamma distribution. In our experiments, we run two days of the trace, corresponding to a Friday and a Saturday, as well as a few extra hours of cache warm-up time pre-pended.

We also simulate an URL status lookup and update service, which maintains the status of URL pages on the web for fast lookup. The key information maintained includes the content type and crawling information of each URL. If a page URL is dead or its content type changes, the status of such a page needs to be updated. Both online and offline search applications with very high request rates can use such a service. Generally, the majority of URLs does not resolve to any updates after being crawled (read-only URLs), while a small portion requires frequent updating (read/write). We used a daily trace from Ask.com as a simulation guidance for the content modification rate. There are about 25% of URL requests which lead to a status update.

5   Experimental Evaluation

5.1   Evaluation of the Basic Algorithm

In this section, we evaluate the basic power-aware resource allocation algorithm, i.e. the version where only the states of the servers are adjusted. No resource management takes place. We use various hard SLA targets (level #1, #2 and #3) and tune the cluster for either maximization of the energy-efficiency or memory utility. To this end, we evaluate the following systems: 1) a baseline without power management, 2) a system which runs a standard load consolidation algorithm that turns residual servers off (*On/Off*), 3) a system which runs our power-aware resource allocation tuned for maximization of energy savings (*Mixed system*), and 4) a system which runs our allocation algorithm tuned for maximization of the memory allocation (*BA*).

Our cluster consists of 16 nodes, each with a memory capacity of 1GB. We make sure that the system always achieves the target level of performance, such that we can keep the evaluation simple by comparing only the *energy-savings* of each system against the baseline. For each level of performance, we assume that the cpu demand to satisfy the level is proportional to the current load demand, while the memory demand is determined such that each level allows a small degradation in its response time (1-2%, 2-3% and 3-4% in respect), compared to the baseline. The memory demands in particular are: 13GB, 11.6GB and 8.5GB in respect, and they are determined during an offline analysis. The respective per-node memory demands are: 0.81GB, 0.66GB and 0.53GB. We also vary the effective server cpu capacity, which controls the aggressiveness of the consolidation, to levels: 50, 70 and 85% of the max capacity. Each experiment consists of running the internet-search snippet generator trace for one weekday and one weekday.

Table 2 summarizes our results. In general, both the mixed and the barely-alive systems achieve significantly higher savings. The mixed system achieves up to 42% energy savings over the baseline and 24% over the on/off, while the barely-alive system achieves up to 34% energy savings over the baseline and 20% over the on/off. The barely-alive system achieves less energy savings compared to the mixed system, as anticipated, because it does not turn servers off. Yet, all the cluster memory is preserved in this case. As an example, on the weekend

Table 2. Performance-power as a function of CPU load, performance target, and day

	Hard SLA #1		Hard SLA #2		Hard SLA #3	
			Energy Savings [%]			
System(transition threshold)	Weekday	Weekend-day	Weekday	Weekend-day	Weekday	Weekend-day
BA(85%)	26.2	34.2	25	33.1	23.4	31.8
BA(70%)	20.2	29.2	18.8	28.0	17.4	26.9
BA(50%)	12.0	18.6	10.8	17.0	9.7	15.5
On/Off(85%)	13.6	14.3	20.3	23.8	26.3	34.9
On/Off(70%)	10.9	14.3	16.6	23.8	20.5	30.9
On/Off(50%)	6.7	12.2	9.7	16.4	12.5	19.9
Mixed(85%)	30.3	38.4	31.2	40.3	31.4	42.4
Mixed(70%)	23.6	33.4	23.8	35.2	23.5	36.3
Mixed(50%)	14.0	22.4	13.9	22.0	13.8	21.5

day with the SLA set to level #3 and the effective cpu utilization to 85%, the barely-alive system saved 8% less energy compared to the mixed system, with an extra unallocated memory of 0.19GB per server or 13GB for the whole cluster.

This fact has several interesting implications. The extra memory can either be allocated to the running service in order to achieve its soft SLA, be allocated to other applications, or be transitioned to a low-power state. Because we are keeping the latency fixed across our experiments, we cannot quantitatively evaluate the soft SLA. Yet, because the barely-alive system has all the memory of the cluster turned on, these savings are the *lower-bound* achieved by a system which would potentially allocate all the rest of memory to the service. The extra memory can also be allocated to another application. Using an application with a low cpu utilization, we are able to harness the benefit of having yet another application executed with only a minor degradation of the energy savings (for the extra active cpus required by the application). There is also the potential for transitioning part of the memory into a low-power state, assuming the system has the capability to transition memory into a low-power state at a fine grain (e.g. rank or device level). This way the energy savings for the barely-alive system could be deeper than the ones that we calculate here.

5.2   Evaluation of the Full Algorithm

We now evaluate the full power-aware resource allocation algorithm, for the case when two services share the cluster. One of the services is the internet-search snippet generator one, while the second one is either the same or the URL lookup service. We also define two new levels of performance, #4 and #5, with corresponding allocations 6.9GB and 5.4GB. The respective per-node allocations are 0.43GB and 0.34GB. Because both services are cpu intensive, we assume that our algorithm does not have the capability to preserve energy in this case, and so we only evaluate the effectiveness of the algorithm to share the memory between the two services, with respect to their target SLAs. Additionally, we vary the priority of the services (0 or 100%).

Table 3 summarizes our results. From this table, it is obvious that when two instances of the internet-search are hosted, without any priorities, the maximum achievable SLA is level #3, which corresponds to a per-server allocation of about 0.5GB (50% of memory capacity). If one instance has 100% priority and the highest SLA demand (level #1), while the other instance has 0 priority, then the algorithm *fails*, because there is no allocation to yield an acceptable hard SLA

Table 3. Performance for multiple sharing services

Priorities Serv.1:2	SLA target Serv.1	SLA target Serv.2	Achieved SLA 1	Achieved SLA 2
0:0	#3	#3	#3	#3
100:0	#1	#3	#1	fail
100:0	#2	#3	#2	#5
100:0	#3	#3	#3	#3

for the second instance. However, if the first instance lowers its SLA demand to level #2, then the second instance can achieve an SLA of level #5. On the other hand, when we utilize the URL lookup service as the second application, we see that the even when the SLA target for search is set to #1 (about 0.8GB), the URL service does not degrade its latency at all. This is because the hit-rate of this service is robust to a much wider range of allocations, i.e. the hit-rate peaks for all allocations between 0.2 - 1GB, compared to the search service, whose hit-rate to size relationship is logarithmic (the actual curves are omitted for the interest of space).

Discussion. Interestingly, our results identified several trends related to the design of management algorithms for datacenter clusters hosting internet-services. First of all, our results showed that, operating at the resource-level, rather than at the server-level as in standard power management, finer control and deeper energy savings are possible. Additionally, our memory sharing results accentuated that an understanding of the correlation between performance (e.g. hit-rate) and resource allocation, for the critical resources, is important for the design of successful management algorithms. Lastly, we demontrasted the need of developing the various management layers (i.e. power, resource and performance management) holistically, such that it is possible deploy all algorithms, without having their individual designs interfere with one another.

6 Conclusion

In this paper, we addressed the multifaceted problem of managing a cluster's resources and power consumption, when hosting cpu- and memory-intense internet services, by proposing a power-aware resource allocation algorithm for the cpu and the memory. Our trace-based simulations showed that we can optimize a cluster either for energy savings (up to 42% over baseline and 24% over state-of-art), for memory allocation (up to 34% and 20% savings in respect), or for sharing among multiple applications. What is more, we adjusted the request distribution algorithm by making it aware of the power and memory management decisions. Our results motivated that a design with SLA-based dynamic management at the resource level, holistically integrating the rest of management algorithms, has a lot of potential for internet clusters.

References

1. Kozyrakis, C., Kansal, A., Sankar, S., Vaid, K.: Server engineering insights for large-scale online services. IEEE Micro 30, 8–19 (2010)
2. Meisner, D., Sadler, C.M., Barroso, L.A., Weber, W.D., Wenisch, T.F.: Power management of online data-intensive services. In: Proceedings of the 38th ISCA, pp. 319–330. ACM, New York (2011)
3. Elnozahy, E.N.M., Kistler, J.J., Rajamony, R.: Energy-Efficient Server Clusters. In: Falsafi, B., VijayKumar, T.N. (eds.) PACS 2002. LNCS, vol. 2325, pp. 179–196. Springer, Heidelberg (2003)

4. Rajamani, K., Lefurgy, C.: On Evaluating Request-Distribution Schemes for Saving Energy in Server Clusters. In: Proceedings of the 2003 IEEE ISPASS, pp. 111–122. IEEE Computer Society, Washington, DC (2003)
5. Bianchini, R., Rajamony, R.: Power and Energy Management for Server Systems (2003)
6. Chen, Y., Das, A., Qin, W., Sivasubramaniam, A., Wang, Q., Gautam, N.: Managing Server Energy and Operational Costs in Hosting Centers. In: SIGMETRICS (2005)
7. Heath, T., Diniz, B., Carrera, E., Meira Jr., W., Bianchini, R.: Energy Conservation in Heterogeneous Server Clusters. In: PPoPP (2005)
8. Pai, V.S., Aron, M., Banga, G., Svendsen, M., Druschel, P., Zwaenepoel, W., Nahum, E.: Locality-aware request distribution in cluster-based network servers. In: Proceedings of the 8th ASPLOS Conference, pp. 205–216. ACM, New York (1998)
9. Carrera, E.V., Bianchini, R.: Press: A clustered server based on user-level communication. IEEE Trans. Parallel Distrib. Syst. 16, 385–395 (2005)
10. Rolia, J., Andrzejak, A., Arlitt, M.: Automating enterprise application placement in resource utilities (2003)
11. Raghavendra, R., Ranganathan, P., Talwar, V., Wang, Z., Zhu, X.: No "power" struggles: coordinated multi-level power management for the data center. SIGARCH Comput. Archit. News 36, 48–59 (2008)
12. Meisner, D., Gold, B.T., Wenisch, T.F.: PowerNap: Eliminating Server Idle Power. In: ASPLOS (2009)
13. Agarwal, Y., et al.: Somniloquy: Augmenting Network Interfaces to Reduce PC Energy Usage. In: NSDI (2009)
14. Anagnostopoulou, V., Biswas, S., Savage, A., Bianchini, R., Yang, T., Chong, F.T.: Energy conservation in datacenters through cluster memory management and barely-alive memory servers. In: Proceedings of the 2009 Workshop on Energy Efficient Design (2009)
15. Zhou, P., Pandey, V., Sundaresan, J., Raghuraman, A., Zhou, Y., Kumar, S.: Dynamic tracking of page miss ratio curve for memory management. In: Proceedings of the 11th ASPLOS-XI, pp. 177–188. ACM, New York (2004)
16. Mattson, R.L., Gescei, J., Slutz, D., Traiger, I.: Evaluation Techniques for Storage Hierarchies. IBM Systems Journal 9(2) (1970)
17. Qureshi, M.K., Patt, Y.N.: Utility-based cache partitioning: A low-overhead, high-performance, runtime mechanism to partition shared caches. In: Proceedings of the 39th IEEE/ACM MICRO Conference, pp. 423–432. IEEE Computer Society, Washington, DC (2006)
18. Barroso, L.A., Hölzle, U.: The Case for Energy-Proportional Computing. IEEE Computer 40(12) (2007)

Exploiting VM Migration for the Automated Power and Performance Management of Green Cloud Computing Systems*

Marco Guazzone, Cosimo Anglano, and Massimo Canonico

Department of Science and Innovation Technology
University of Piemonte Orientale
Alessandria, Italy
{marco.guazzone,cosimo.anglano,massimo.canonico}@mfn.unipmn.it

Abstract. Cloud computing is an emerging computing paradigm in which "Everything is as a Service", including the provision of virtualized computing infrastructures (known as *Infrastructure-as-a-Service* modality) hosted on the physical infrastructure, owned by an infrastructure provider. The goal of this infrastructure provider is to maximize its profit by minimizing the amount of violations of *Quality-of-Service* (QoS) levels agreed with its customers and, at the same time, by lowering infrastructure costs among which energy consumption plays a major role. In this paper, we propose a framework able to automatically manage resources of cloud infrastructures in order to simultaneously achieve suitable QoS levels and to reduce as much as possible the amount of energy used for providing services. We show, through simulation, that our approach is able to dynamically adapt to time-varying workloads (without any prior knowledge) and to significantly reduce QoS violations and energy consumption with respect to traditional static approaches.

Keywords: Cloud computing, Green computing, SLA.

1 Introduction

The *Cloud Computing* [1] paradigm has enabled various novel modalities of service provisioning. Among them, particularly important is the *Infrastructure-as-a-Service* (IaaS) modality, whereby an *Infrastructure Customer* (IC) may provision his/her own virtual computing infrastructure, on which (s)he can deploy and run arbitrary software, on top on the physical infrastructure owned by an *Infrastructure Provider* (IP). Typically, ICs deploy on their virtual infrastructure multi-tier distributed applications consisting in an ensemble of *Virtual Machines* (VMs), each one hosting one or more application components together with the corresponding operating environment (i.e., OS and software libraries, just to name a few).

Usually, the IC and the IP agree on *Quality-of-Service* (QoS) levels that the IP commits to deliver to applications, which are defined in terms of suitable low-level temporal

---

* This work was supported in part by the Italian Research Ministry under the PRIN 2008 *Energy eFFIcient teChnologIEs for the Networks of Tomorrow* (EFFICIENT) project.

J. Huusko et al. (Eds.): E^{2}DC 2012, LNCS 7396, pp. 81–92, 2012.

and performance metrics commonly referred to as *Service Level Objectives* (SLO). This agreement, commonly referred to as *Service Level Agreement* (SLA), usually states that the IC accepts to pay a certain amount of money for using the infrastructure, and that the IP accepts to pay a money penalty for each violation of the SLA.

A critical issue that the IP must solve in order to maximize revenues is the amount of physical resources that must be allocated to each application. On the one hand, the allocation of an insufficient amount of resources may indeed yield a large number of SLA violations, with consequent losses due to corresponding money penalties. On the other hand, the allocation of an excessive amount of resources typically results in increases of energy costs, caused by a larger number of switched-on resources. These costs represent, at the moment, a large fraction of the *Total Cost of Ownership* (TCO) of the infrastructure [2], and are expected to further grow in the near future. Ideally, therefore, the IP should be able to allocate to each IC application no more than the minimum amount of resources resulting in no SLA violation, in order to keep the energy consumption to a bare minimum.

The standard approach generally adopted to allocate physical resources to the VMs of an application consists in statically assigning to each one of them enough capacity to fulfill the SLAs under the hypothesis that the workload will exhibit a specific intensity. This approach, however, fails to provide satisfactory results in realistic settings, because of the following factors:

- The characteristics of the workload are rarely known in advance, so it is very hard (if not impossible) to estimate its typical intensity. The resulting estimation errors lead to either under-provisioning (with consequent SLA violations) or over-provisioning of resources (with consequent energy waste).
- The intensity of the workload typically changes over time, so even if (unrealistically) the value of the intensity could be estimated without errors, the capacity allocated to the VMs should be dynamically adapted to these changes. This adaptation, however, may not be possible for a VM if the physical resource on which it is running has no spare capacity left, an event that is likely to occur in realistic settings where each physical resource is typically shared among many competing VMs, that usually exhibit different and conflicting resource utilization profiles.
- The VMs of the same application usually span different physical resources, that are all involved by the above adaptation, with the consequence that changes in the allocation of capacity to a given application create a domino effect involving a large set of other applications.

In order to tackle the problem of allocating the resources of a cloud physical infrastructure in face of the above issues, in [3] we proposed a distributed, time-hierarchical resource management framework that aims at simultaneously minimize SLA violations and energy consumption for multi-tier applications characterized by time-varying workloads whose characteristics are unknown in advance.

The framework encompasses three distinct levels, that operate on different system components at different time-scale, namely:

- an *Application Manager* for each application, that exploits control-theoretic techniques to monitor its SLOs, and dynamically determine the physical resource share that must be allocated to each of its VMs in order to meet the corresponding SLAs;

- a *Physical Machine Manager* for each physical resource, that multiplexes the total amount of physical capacity among all the VMs allocated on that resource;
- a *Migration Manager*, that monitors the SLOs of all applications and the overall energy consumption, and decides whether it is appropriate to migrate some VMs from the physical machines where they are allocated to other ones, in order to meet their SLAs and save energy.

In [3], we focused on the design and evaluation of the Application Manager and the Physical Machine Manager, and we showed that, when the workload is such that each physical machine has enough capacity to accommodate the simultaneous needs of all the VMs allocated on it, our framework results both in better performance and lower energy consumption than alternative static approaches.

This paper focuses instead on the Migration Manager. In particular, we present its architecture, the algorithms it uses, and a performance evaluation study carried out by means of *discrete-event simulation* [4], whereby we assess its ability to respect SLAs and save energy by comparing the performance attained by our framework when migration is enabled against those attained when migration is disabled, and against various static resource management approaches.

The rest of this paper is organized as follows. In Sect. 2, after a brief recap of our framework, we describe the Migration Manager. In Sect. 3, we present an experimental evaluation of our framework and show its effectiveness on minimizing SLO violations and energy consumption. In Sect. 4, we compare our approach with some recent related work. Finally, in Sect. 5, we conclude this paper and present future works.

2   The Resource Management Framework

The architecture of our framework includes a certain number of multi-tier applications which have to be deployed on a cloud infrastructure. Every application tier is deployed in a separate VM, which in turn is placed on one of the available Physical Machines (PMs). The core of our framework is the *Resource Manager*, which continuously monitors the performance of each deployed application and suitably acts on the system in order to maintain application performance goals and, at the same time, to minimize the energy consumption of computing resources.

We assume that the SLOs of each application are known, and are expressed in terms of a specific PM that we called *reference machine*.[1] It is responsibility of the Resource Manager to appropriately scale SLOs according to the capacity of physical resources belonging to the PMs where each application tier is actually run. To do so, we assume that the relative computing power (i.e., the measure of how much a physical resource is more powerful than another one) of two PMs of the same category can be expressed by a simple proportional relationship between their capacities. This means that if a resource has capacity of 10, it will be able to serve requests at a service rate double than a resource with capacity of 5.

---

[1] This choice appears to be natural, as (1) application performance generally vary according to the capacity of physical resources assigned to that application, and (2) physical resources inside cloud computing systems are usually heterogeneous.

In order to reduce energy consumption and achieve application performance targets, the Resource Manager exploits virtualization technologies and control-theoretic techniques. On the one hand, by deploying each application tier inside a separate VM, virtualization provides both a runtime isolated environment and a mean for dynamically provisioning physical resources to virtualized applications so that an effective use of physical resources can be achieved. On the other hand, control theory provides a way for enabling computing systems to automatically manage performance and power consumption, without human intervention. Thus, the Resource Manager accomplishes its goal by dynamically adjusting the fraction of the capacity of PMs assigned to each VM, and, if needed, by migrating one or more VMs into other and more appropriated PMs (possibly, by turning on or off some of them). Specifically, it acts on the cloud infrastructure via a set of independent components, namely *Application Manager*, *Physical Machine Manager*, and *Migration Manager*.

In the rest of this section we describe the Migration Manager, which is the focus of this paper. For the other two components, the interested reader may refer to [3] for a more thorough description. We just want to recall that the Application and the Physical Machine Managers act on a short-term time scale, and attempt to allocate, to the various tiers of each application, the share of physical resources they need to meet their SLOs.

It is worth noting that, although our framework is general enough to deal with any type of physical resource and performance metric, for the sake of simplicity, in this paper we restrict our focus to the CPU as the type of shared physical resource, and on the application-level response time, as the SLO performance metric.

2.1   The Migration Manager

The purpose of the Migration Manager is to find the placement of the currently running VMs on the PMs that results in the minimization of both SLO violations and energy consumption. This objective is achieved by monitoring application performance and by recomputing, if needed, a new VM placement that simultaneously results in the fulfillment of SLOs and in the lowest energy consumption among all the candidate ones. The new placement is computed at the end of regularly-spaced time intervals henceforth referred to as *control intervals*.

Once the optimal allocation is computed, the following (non-mutually exclusive) actions can be triggered: (1) one or more PMs are powered on in order to fulfill current CPU demand, (2) one or more VMs are migrated to more suitable PMs, and (3) one or more PMs are powered off due to an excess of available CPU capacity with respect to current demand.

The optimal allocation is computed by solving, at each control interval k, an optimization problem, whose mathematical formulation (the *mathematical program*) is shown in Fig. 1, where M and V denote the set of all PMs of the cloud infrastructure (included the ones currently powered off), and the set of all virtual machines that are currently powered on, respectively, and $x_i(\cdot)$, $y_{ij}(\cdot)$, and $s_{ij}(\cdot)$ are the decision variables. More details about the mathematical program are provided in [5].

Solution Algorithm. The above mathematical program is a *Mixed-Integer Nonlinear Program* (MINLP) [6] which is known to be NP-hard [7]. Thus, we resorted to an ap-

minimize

$$J(k) = \left[\frac{1}{g_e} \sum_{i \in M} W_i(k) x_i(k) \right.$$

$$+ \frac{1}{g_m} \sum_{i \in M} \sum_{h \in M} \sum_{j \in V} \pi_{jhi}(k) y_{hj}(k-1) y_{ij}(k) \tag{1a}$$

$$\left. + \frac{1}{g_p} \sum_{i \in M} \sum_{j \in V} y_{ij}(k) \left(s_{ij}(k) - \hat{s}_{ij}(k) \right)^2 \right]$$

subject to

$$x_i(k) \in \{0, 1\}, \qquad\qquad\qquad i \in M, \tag{1b}$$

$$y_{ij}(k) \in \{0, 1\}, \qquad\qquad\qquad i \in M, j \in V, \tag{1c}$$

$$s_{ij}(k) \in [0, 1], \qquad\qquad\qquad i \in M, j \in V, \tag{1d}$$

$$\sum_{i \in M} y_{ij}(k) = 1, \qquad\qquad\qquad j \in V, \tag{1e}$$

$$y_{ij}(k) \le x_i(k), \qquad\qquad\qquad i \in M, j \in V, \tag{1f}$$

$$x_i(k) \le \sum_{j \in V} y_{ij}(k), \qquad\qquad\qquad i \in M, \tag{1g}$$

$$s_{ij}(k) \le y_{ij}(k), \qquad\qquad\qquad i \in M, j \in V, \tag{1h}$$

$$s_{ij}(k) \frac{C_i}{\bar{C}} \ge y_{ij}(k) \bar{s}_{t_j}^{\min}, \qquad\qquad\qquad i \in M, j \in V, \tag{1i}$$

$$\sum_{j \in V} s_{ij}(k) \le s_i^{\max}, \qquad\qquad\qquad i \in M, \tag{1j}$$

$$\hat{u}_i(k) \le u_i^{\max}, \qquad\qquad\qquad i \in M. \tag{1k}$$

Fig. 1. Resource management framework – Optimization problem for the Migration Manager

proximate solution computed by means of a *Best-Fit Decreasing* (BFD) strategy, which attempts to place the largest number of VMs on the fewest number of PMs, while still preserving SLO constraints. More details can be found in [5].

3   Experimental Evaluation

In order to assess the capability of our framework, we performed an extensive experimental evaluation using discrete-event simulation. To this end, we developed a C++ ad-hoc discrete-event system simulator, that is used to run our experiments.

We assess the performance of our framework by measuring, for each application, its response time and the number of SLO violations, as well as the amount of electrical energy (in Joule) consumed by the physical infrastructure. For each of these quantities, we compute the 95% confidence level by using the *independent replications* output analysis, where the length of each replication is fixed to $210,000$ ticks of simulated time, and the number of total replicas is fixed to 5. We use these fixed settings since the simulated system never reaches the steady-state due to the presence of applications that can start and stop in the middle of the simulation.

In our experiments, we use the 0.99^{th} quantile of application response time as SLO specification. This means that the infrastructure provider will pay penalties only when the percentage of SLO violations (i.e., the percentage of the number of times the observed response time is larger than the SLO value) is greater than 1% during a prescribed time interval.

To compute the SLO value for each application, we use a benchmark-like approach similar to the one described in [8,9] for application profiling: for each type of application and arrival process, we run a series of simulations (assigning to each tier exactly the amount of CPU capacity as defined by the reference machine specifications) and measure the 0.99^{th} quantile of the response time empirical distribution.

In the rest of this section, we first present the settings used to define the various simulation scenarios used for our study, and then we report and discuss the results obtained from the experiments.

3.1 Experimental Settings

The experimental scenarios are defined in terms of the configurations of the physical infrastructure and of the various applications, and of the specific settings for the parameters used by the various components of the framework.

Table 1. Experimental settings – Characteristics of the PMs and applications

(a) Characteristcs of the PMs.

Group	No. of PMs	CPU Capacity	ω_0	ω_1	ω_2	ρ
M_1	3	1,000	86.7	119.1	69.06	0.400
M_2	2	2,000	143.0	258.2	117.2	0.355
M_3	2	3,000	178.0	310.6	160.4	0.311
M_4	2	4,000	284.0	490.1	343.7	0.462

(b) Characteristics of the applications.

Group	1st Tier	2nd Tier	3rd Tier
A_1	0.060	0.06	0.06
A_2	0.030	0.06	0.03
A_3	0.015	0.03	0.06

Physical Infrastructure Configuration. We consider a cloud infrastructure consisting of a set of 9 heterogeneous PMs, that, in turn, are divided into 4 groups, namely M_1, M_2, M_3, and M_4, in such a way that the PMs in the same group M_i have an identical CPU capacity that is i times larger than the one of the reference machine (that is assumed to be equal to 1,000).

The energy consumption of these machines is modeled as discussed in [10,11,12], whereby the power P absorbed by each machine is related to its CPU utilization u by means of the formula:

$$P = \omega_0 + \omega_1 u + \omega_2 u^\rho \qquad (2)$$

where ω_0, ω_1 and ω_2 are model parameters. For each one of the machine classes, we use a different setting of the parameters in Equation (2) (that is used for all the machines in the same class), as reported in Table 1a (where we also report the capacity values and the number of PMs for each of the four machine groups). These values are estimated through a statistical regression analysis over data collected by the *SPECpower_ssj2008* benchmark [13].

Application Configuration. We consider 6 three-tier applications divided into 3 groups, namely A_1, A_2, and A_3, such that applications in the same group have an identical behavior. For every application, each incoming service request arrives at the first tier that, after processing it, forwards it to the second tier where this process is repeated. Finally, after the processing in the third tier has taken place, the result of the service request is sent back to the respective client. These application classes differ from each other in the amount of processing time requested by each tier (expressed in terms of the computing power of the reference machine), as reported in Table 1b.

Each application is characterized by its workload, that consists in a stream of service requests, continuously generated by a population of users of unknown size, arriving according to a specific arrival process. In order to reproduce various operating conditions that may occur for real-world applications, we consider three different request arrival processes, namely:

- *Deterministic Modulated Poisson Process* (DMPP), to generate workloads exhibiting user behavioral patterns like daily-cycles of activity. In particular, we consider a three-state DMPP, henceforth denoted as $DMPP(\lambda_1, \lambda_2, \lambda_3, \tau)$, where λ_i, for $i = 1, \ldots, 3$, is the arrival rate of the Poisson process in state i, and τ is the deterministic state-residence time;
- *Pareto Modulated Poisson Process* (PMPP) [14] to generate self-similar workloads. In particular, we consider a two-states PMPP, from this time forth denoted as $PMPP(\lambda_1, \lambda_2, x_m, \alpha)$, where λ_i, for $i = 1, 2$, is the arrival rate of the Poisson process in state i, and x_m and α are the minimum value and shape parameters of the Pareto distribution, respectively;
- *Markov Modulated Poisson Process* (MMPP) [15] to generate arrival processes exhibiting temporal burstiness [16]. In particular, we consider a two-states MMPP, henceforth denoted as $MMPP(\lambda_1, \lambda_2, \mu_1, \mu_2)$, where λ_i, for $i = 1, 2$, is the arrival rate of the Poisson process in state i, and μ_i, for $i = 1, 2$, is the state-transition rate when the process is in state i.

Starting from these arrival processes, we create four distinct application scenarios, each one including six instances of applications: three *persistent* instances (henceforth denoted as Per_1, Per_2, and Per_3) whose lifetime spans the entire simulation, and three *ephemeral* instances (henceforth denoted as Eph_1, Eph_2, and Eph_3) that arrive in the system at different instants (i.e., time $10,000$, $70,000$, and $130,000$, respectively), and leave $70,000$ time units after their arrival. The details of the four scenarios considered in our experiments, together with the SLOs of each application in each scenario, are reported in Table 2.

Resource Manager Configuration. The parameters characterizing the Resource Manager (see Sect. 2) include the ones associated to each Application Manager, Physical Machine Manager, and to the Migration Manager. Due to lack of space, we omit them from this paper. For more details, the interested reader can refer to [5].

3.2 Results and Discussion

In order to assess the effectiveness of the Migration Manager, we compare it with the following resource management static policies:

- STATIC-SLO: each VM (running a specific application tier) is assigned the amount of CPU capacity $Cap(SLO)$ needed to meet application SLOs, so that SLOs satisfaction is favoured over energy consumption reduction;
- STATIC-ENERGY: each VM is statically assigned a fixed amount of capacity that is 25% lower than $Cap(SLO)$. This is an energy-conserving approach since, by assigning less capacity than required, energy consumption reduction is given priority over SLOs satisfaction;
- STATIC-TRADEOFF: each VM is assigned a fixed amount of capacity that is 10% lower than $Cap(SLO)$, in order to seek a reasonable trade-off between energy consumption reduction and SLOs preservation.

It should be noted that all these policies are based on the rather unrealistic assumption that $Cap(SLO)$ is exactly known, whose knowledge requires the ability to perform measurement experiments during which each application is exposed to its workload for a suitable amount of time.

Table 2. Experimental settings – Arrival process parameters and SLO values of the applications. For each scenario, but the S-MIX one, the arrival process is the same as the one implied by the scenario name. In S-MIX, the arrival process is DMPP for A_1, MMPP for A_2 and PMPP for A_3.

| Scenario | Application | | | | | |
| | A_1 | | A_2 | | A_3 | |
	Arrival	SLO	Arrival	SLO	Arrival	SLO
S-DMPP	$(1,5,10,3600)$	1.176	$(10,5,1,3600)$	0.612	$(5,10,1,3600)$	0.608
S-PMPP	$(5,10,1,1.5)$	1.245	$(5,10,1,1.5)$	0.655	$(5,10,1,1.5)$	0.624
S-MMPP	$(5,15,0.0002,0.002)$	4.001	$(5,15,0.0002,0.002)$	1.962	$(5,15,0.0002,0.002)$	1.935
S-MIX	$(5,10,1,3600)$	0.608	$(5,15,0.0002,0.002)$	1.935	$(5,10,1,1.5)$	0.624

Moreover, in order to assess the benefits of VM migration with respect to situations where only the Application Manager and the Physical Machine Manager are present (as in our previous work [3]), we consider two different variants of our approach, denoted respectively as OUR-APPROACH-NM and OUR-APPROACH-M, which differ in that the former does not use the Migration Manager component (and hence does not employ VM migration).

Our comparison is performed by considering the following performance indices (for each one of them, we compute the 95% confidence intervals):

- *SLO violations*: the mean percentage of SLO violations for each application instance;
- *Total Energy* (TotEn): total amount of electrical energy (measured in kilowatt-hours, kWh) spent to serve all the requests received by applications.
- *Wasted Energy* (WastEn): total amount of electrical energy (measured in kilowatt-hours, kWh) spent to serve out-of-SLO requests (this amount of energy can be, therefore, considered as wasted to serve requests that will imply a money penalty for the provider).

Due to lack of space, we only report part of performed experiments. The interested reader can refer to [5] for a complete discussion of experimental evaluation. The results of the various scenarios are presented in two separate tables, namely Table 3 (for S-PMPP) and Table 4 (for S-MIX). In each table, every column reports the results obtained, by the various applications, under a specific resource management approach (an "n/a" value means that the use of the corresponding resource management approach made the simulation unable to converge).

Table 3. Experimental results – S-PMPP scenario. Energy consumption refers to a period of 210,000 simulated seconds (i.e., approximately 2.5 simulated days).

			Approach				
			STATIC-*			OUR-APPROACH-*	
			SLO	ENERGY	TRADEOFF	NM	M
		Per_1	0.58	19.60	2.57	0.58	0.59
		Eph_1	0.89	33.89	4.17	0.90	0.90
SLO	(%)	Per_2	0.68	16.04	2.68	0.68	0.68
Violations		Eph_2	0.82	9.33	3.24	0.83	0.82
		Per_3	0.53	15.62	2.37	0.53	0.53
		Eph_3	0.47	11.57	1.84	0.47	0.47
Energy	(kWh)	TotEn	109.28	116.46	118.72	107.31	98.27
Consumption		WastEn	0.70	20.65	3.23	0.69	0.63

Table 4. Experimental results – S-MIX scenario. Energy consumption refers to a period of 210,000 simulated seconds (i.e., approximately 2.5 simulated days).

			Approach				
			STATIC-*			OUR-APPROACH-*	
			SLO	ENERGY	TRADEOFF	NM	M
		Per_1	0.81	n/a	3.23	0.81	0.81
		Eph_1	0.79	n/a	3.14	0.79	0.79
SLO	(%)	Per_2	0.87	n/a	20.86	0.84	0.82
Violations		Eph_2	0.44	n/a	15.09	0.51	0.52
		Per_3	0.55	n/a	2.36	0.55	0.56
		Eph_3	0.65	n/a	2.75	0.65	0.66
Energy	(kWh)	TotEn	87.99	n/a	91.41	87.58	82.65
Consumption		WastEn	0.63	n/a	7.12	0.65	0.58

By looking at the results reported in these tables, we can first observe that while both OUR-APPROACH-M and OUR-APPROACH-NM practically result in identical values of SLO violations for all the scenarios, the former always results in a more efficient usage of physical resources. As a matter of fact, OUR-APPROACH-M always results in lower values of TotEn metric: this means that the exploitation of VM migration allows to both save energy (lower TotEn values) and to better use the energy that is consumed (lower WastEn values).

Let us now compare the performance of OUR-APPROACH-M against those attained by the static policies.

As indicated by our results, STATIC-ENERGY and STATIC-TRADEOFF always result in higher values of SLO violations and energy consumption than OUR-APPROACH-M. Furthermore, STATIC-ENERGY can be considered worse than STATIC-TRADEOFF since it results in a moderate improvement of (unit) energy consumption at the price of much higher values of SLO violations. Therefore, we can conclude that our approach is able to satisfy SLOs for a greater number of requests with a lower energy consumption and, more importantly, without resulting in any penalty to be paid by the provider, than these two static approaches.

The comparison with the STATIC-SLO policy needs more attention. First of all, we can observe that OUR-APPROACH-M practically exhibits the same values of SLO violations than STATIC-SLO for all the scenarios. For this latter scenario, OUR-APPROACH-M results in a higher number of SLO violations only for the Per_1 application, while, for the remaining applications, this metric practically exhibits the same values.

If, however, we look at the efficiency-related metrics, we can observe that OUR-APPROACH-M always results in lower values of TotEn and WastEn than STATIC-SLO, indicating that the former is able to consume less energy and to use physical resources more effectively. Moreover, it is important to observe that STATIC-SLO, in addition to be unrealistic, requires an overcommitment of resources, whereby a larger fraction of CPU capacity is assigned to each VM regardless of the fact that this fraction will be actually used by the VM. As a result, this implies that the number of VMs that can be consolidated on the same PM is lower than those attained by our approach (that, instead, allocates to each VM just the fraction of CPU capacity it needs). Therefore, STATIC-SLO potentially requires, for a given number of VMs, a larger number of physical resources than the our approach one, thus yielding a larger energy consumption.

4   Related Works

The problem of dynamically managing physical resources of a cloud infrastructure in such a way to take into consideration both performance targets of hosted applications and power consumption of the infrastructure has been studied in the literature only recently.

In [17], a series of adaptive algorithms for dynamic VM consolidation are proposed and evaluated. Unlike this work, our solution, has a decentralized architecture and, through the combination of online system identification and VM migration, is able to work with any type of workload.

In [18], a combined predictive and reactive provisioning technique is proposed, where the predictive component estimates the needed fraction of capacity according to historical workload trace analysis, while the reactive component is used to handle workload excess with respect to the analyzed one. Unlike this work, our solution, by means of online system identification, is potentially able to work with any type of workload without any prior knowledge.

In [19], an online resource provisioning framework is proposed for combined power and performance management as a sequential multi-objective optimization problem under uncertainty and is solved using limited lookahead control, which is a form of model predictive control [20]. The key difference between this work and our approach is in the type of the architectural design adopted: centralized for the former, and decentralized for the latter. It is important to note that authors also show, via trace-driven simulation, that the use of a feed-forward neural network can make their work potentially able to scale to large systems. Unfortunately, the lack of details makes us unable to perform any sort of comparison.

In [21], a two-layers hierarchical control approach is proposed. Even though this work shares some architectural similarity with our framework, there are two important differences; the first difference is in the way parameters of the black-box application model (i.e., ARX) are computed (i.e., through offline identification), while the second one is in the way CPU shares are assigned to application tiers (which is not well suited for situations where tiers of different applications are hosted on the same PM).

Finally, in [22], a two-levels control architecture is proposed, where, unlike our approach, the achievement of performance targets is always subjected to the reduction of power consumption; conversely, in our approach, the reduction of power consumption is constrained to the achievement of performance targets.

5   Conclusions

In this paper, we presented a framework for automatically managing computing resources of cloud computing infrastructures, in order to simultaneously satisfy SLO constraints and reduce system-level energy consumption, that exploits VM migration to obtain its goals. By means of simulation, we showed that, compared to traditional static approaches, our framework is able to dynamically adapt to time-varying workloads (with no prior knowledge) and, at the same time, to significantly reduce both SLO violations and energy consumption. Furthermore, we showed that VM migration actually results in significant performance and energy consumption improvements over situations where the same framework does not use VM migration.

There are several avenues of research that we plan to explore in the near future. First of all, we would like to extend the framework to also take into consideration other resource types (e.g., memory and disks) and system components (e.g. network routers and switches). Furthermore, we would like to extend the framework in such a way to enable it to manage federations of cloud infrastructures. Finally, we plan to integrate it into a cloud management middleware in order to test it under real operating conditions.

References

1. Weiss, A.: Computing in the clouds. netWorker 11(4), 16–25 (2007)
2. ENERGY STAR Program: Report to congress on server and data center energy efficiency. Technical report, U.S. EPA (August 2007)
3. Guazzone, M., et al.: Energy-efficient resource management for cloud computing infrastructures. In: Proc. of the 3rd IEEE Int. Conf. on Cloud Computing Technology and Science (CloudCom 2011) (2011)
4. Banks, J., et al.: Discrete-Event System Simulation, 5th edn. Prentice Hall (2010)

5. Guazzone, M., et al.: Exploiting VM migration for the automated power and performance management of green cloud computing systems. Technical Report TR-INF-2012-04-02-UNIPMN, University of Piemonte Orientale (April 2012)
6. Lee, J., et al. (eds.): Mixed Integer Nonlinear Programming. The IMA Volumes in Mathematics and its Applications, vol. 154. Springer Science+Business Media, LLC (2012)
7. Jeroslow, R.: There cannot be any algorithm for integer programming with quadratic constraints. Oper. Res. 21(1), 221–224 (1973)
8. Yang, L.T., et al.: Cross-platform performance prediction of parallel applications using partial execution. In: Proc. of the 2005 ACM/IEEE Conference on Supercomputing, SC 2005 (2005)
9. Wood, T., et al.: Profiling and Modeling Resource Usage of Virtualized Applications. In: Issarny, V., Schantz, R. (eds.) Middleware 2008. LNCS, vol. 5346, pp. 366–387. Springer, Heidelberg (2008)
10. Beloglazov, A., et al.: A taxonomy and survey of energy-efficient data centers and cloud computing systems. In: Zelkowitz, M.V. (ed.) Advances in Computers, vol. 82, pp. 47–111. Elsevier (2011)
11. Fan, X., et al.: Power provisioning for a warehouse-sized computer. In: Proc. of the 34th Int. Symp. on Computer Architecture (ISCA 2007), pp. 13–23 (2007)
12. Rivoire, S., et al.: A comparison of high-level full-system power models. In: Proc. of the 2008 USENIX Conf. on Power Aware Computing and Systems (HotPower 2008), pp. 1–5 (2008)
13. Standard Performance Evaluation Corporation: SPECpower_ssj2008 benchmark, http://www.spec.org/power_ssj2008
14. Le-Ngoc, T., et al.: A Pareto-modulated Poisson process (PMPP) model for long-range dependent traffic. Comput. Comm. 23(2), 123–132 (2000)
15. Fischer, W., et al.: The Markov-modulated Poisson Process (MMPP) cookbook. Perform. Eval. 18(2), 149–171 (1993)
16. Mi, N., et al.: Injecting realistic burstiness to a traditional client-server benchmark. In: Proc. of the 6th IEEE Int. Conf. on Autonomic Computing (ICAC 2009), pp. 149–158 (2009)
17. Beloglazov, A., et al.: Optimal online deterministic algorithms and adaptive heuristics for energy and performance efficient dynamic consolidation of virtual machines in Cloud data centers. Concurrency Comput. Pract. Ex. (accepted for publication)
18. Gandhi, A., et al.: Minimizing data center SLA violations and power consumption via hybrid resource provisioning. In: Proc. of the 2nd Int. Green Computing Conf., IGCC 2010 (2011)
19. Kusic, D., et al.: Combined power and performance management of virtualized computing environments serving session-based workloads. IEEE Trans. on Netw. and Serv. Manag. 8(3), 245–258 (2011)
20. Camacho, E.F., et al.: Model Predictive Control, 2nd edn. Springer (2004)
21. Xiong, P., et al.: Economical and robust provisioning of n-tier cloud workloads: A multi-level control approach. In: Proc. of the 31st Int. Conf. on Distributed Computing Systems (ICDCS 2011), pp. 571–580 (2011)
22. Wang, X., et al.: Coordinating power control and performance management for virtualized server clusters. IEEE Trans. Parallel Distrib. Syst. 22(2), 245–259 (2011)

Energy Efficient Service Delivery in Clouds in Compliance with the Kyoto Protocol

Drazen Lucanin[1,2], Michael Maurer[1], Toni Mastelic[1], and Ivona Brandic[1]

[1] Vienna Univ. of Technology, Vienna, Austria
{drazen,maurer,toni,ivona}@infosys.tuwien.ac.at
[2] Ruder Boskovic Inst., Zagreb, Croatia

Abstract. Cloud computing is revolutionizing the ICT landscape by providing scalable and efficient computing resources on demand. The ICT industry – especially data centers, are responsible for considerable amounts of CO_2 emissions and will very soon be faced with legislative restrictions, such as the Kyoto protocol, defining caps at different organizational levels (country, industry branch etc.) A lot has been done around energy efficient data centers, yet there is very little work done in defining flexible models considering CO_2. In this paper we present a first attempt of modeling data centers in compliance with the Kyoto protocol. We discuss a novel approach for trading credits for emission reductions across data centers to comply with their constraints. CO_2 caps can be integrated with Service Level Agreements and juxtaposed to other computing commodities (e.g. computational power, storage), setting a foundation for implementing next-generation schedulers and pricing models that support Kyoto-compliant CO_2 trading schemes.

1 Introduction

With the global advent of cloud, grid, cluster computing and increasing needs for large data centers to run these services, the environmental impact of large-scale computing paradigms is becoming a global problem. The energy produced to power the ICT industry (and data centers constitute its major part) is responsible for 2% of all the carbon dioxide equivalent (CO_2e – greenhouse gases normalized to carbon dioxide by their environmental impact) emissions [6], thus accelerating global warming [11].

Cloud computing facilitate users to buy computing resources from a cloud provider and specify the exact amount of each resource (such as storage space, number of cores etc.) that they expect through a Service Level Agreement (SLA)[1]. The cloud provider then honors this agreement by providing the promised resources to avoid agreement violation penalties (and to keep the customer satisfied to continue doing business). However, cloud providers are usually faced with the challenge of satisfying promised SLAs and at the same time not

---

[1] We consider the traditional business model where the desired specifications are set in advance, as is still the case in most infrastructure-as-a-service clouds.

J. Huusko et al. (Eds.): E^{2}DC 2012, LNCS 7396, pp. 93–104, 2012.

wasting their resources as a user very rarely utilizes computing resources to the maximum [14].

In order to fight global warming the Kyoto protocol was established by the United Nations Framework Convention on Climate Change (UNFCCC or FCCC). The goal is to achieve global stabilisation of greenhouse gas concentrations in the atmosphere at a level that would prevent dangerous anthropogenic interference with the climate system [13]. The protocol defines control mechanisms to reduce CO_2e emissions by basically setting a market price for such emissions. Currently, flexible models for CO_2e trading are developed at different organizational and political level as for example at the level of a country, industry branch, or a company. As a result, keeping track of and reducing CO_2e emissions is becoming more and more relevant after the ratification of the Kyoto protocol.

Energy efficiency has often been a target for research. On the one hand, there is large body of work done in facilitating energy efficient management of data centers as for example in [8] where current state of formal energy efficiency control in cloud computing relies on monitoring power usage efficiency (PUE) and the related family of metrics developed by the Green Grid Consortium. Another example is discussed in [15] where economic incentives are presented to promote greener cloud computing policies. On the other hand, there are several mature models for trading CO_2e obligations in various industrial branches, as for example in the oil industry [17]. Surprisingly, to the best of our knowledge there exists no related work about the application of the Kyoto protocol to energy efficient modeling of data centers and cloud infrastructures.

In this paper we propose a CO_2e-trading model for transparent scheduling of resources in cloud computing adhering to the Kyoto protocol guidelines [17]. First, we present a conceptual model for CO_2e trading compliant to the Kyoto protocol's emission trading scheme. We consider an *emission trading market (ETM)* where *credits for emission reduction (CERs)* are traded between data centers. Based on the positive or negative *CERs* of the data center, a cost is set for the environmental impact of the energy used by applications. Thereby, a successful application scheduing decission can be brought after considering the (i) energy costs, (ii) CO_2e costs and (iii) SLA violation costs. Second, we propose a *wastage-penalty* model that can be used as a basis for the implementation of Kyoto protocol-compliant scheduling and pricing models. Finally, we discuss potential uses of the model as an optimisation heuristic in the resource scheduler.

The main contribution of the paper are (1) definition of the conceptual *emission trading market (ETM)* for the application of Kyoto protocol for the energy efficiency management in Clouds (2) definition of a *wastage - penalty* model for trading of *credits for emission reduction (CERs)* (3) discussion on how the presented *wastage-penalty* model can be used for the implementation of next generation Kyoto protocol compliant energy efficient schedulers and pricing models.

The paper is structured as follows: Section 2 discusses related work. Section 3 gives some background as to why cloud computing might become subject to the Kyoto protocol. Section 4 presents our model in a general CO_2e-trading cloud scenario, we then go on to define a formal model of individual costs to find a theoretical balance and discuss the usefulness of such a model as a scheduling heuristic. Section 5 concludes the paper and identifies possible future research directions.

2   Related Work

As our aim is to enable energy efficiency control in the cloud resource scheduling domain, there are two groups of work related to ours that deal with the problem:

1. scheduling algorithms - resource allocation techniques, from which energy cost optimisation is starting to evolve
2. energy efficiency legislation - existing rules, regulations and best behaviour suggestions that are slowly moving from optimising the whole data center efficiency towards optimising its constituting parts

We will examine each of these two groups separately now.

2.1   Scheduling Algorithms

There already exist cloud computing energy efficient scheduling solutions, such as [21,20] which try to minimize energy consumption, but they lack a strict quantitative model similar to PUE that would be convenient as a legislative control measure to express exactly how much they alter CO_2e emission levels. From the CO_2e management perspective, these methods work more in a best-effort manner, attempting first and foremost to satisfy SLA constrains.

In [16] the HGreen heuristic is proposed to schedule batch jobs on the greenest resource first, based on prior energy efficiency benchmarking of all the nodes, but not how to optimize a job once it is allocated to a node - how much of its resources is it allowed to consume. A similar multiple-node-oriented scheduling algorithm is presented in [22].

The work described in [15] has the most similarities with ours, since it also balances SLA and energy constraints and even describes energy consumption using a similar, linear model motivated by dynamic voltage scaling, but no consideration of CO_2e management was made inside the model.

A good overview of cloud computing and sustainability is given in [18], with explanations of where cloud computing stands in regard to CO_2e emissions. Green policies for scheduling are proposed that, if accepted by the user, could greatly increase the efficiency of cloud computing and reduce CO_2e emissions. Reducing emissions is not treated as a source of profit and a possible way to balance SLA violations, though, but more of a general guideline for running the data center to stay below a certain threshold.

2.2   Energy Efficiency Legislation

Measures of controlling energy efficiency in data centers do exist – metrics such as power usage efficiency (PUE) [10], carbon usage efficiency (CUE), water usage efficiency (WUE) [9] and others have basically become the industry standards through the joint efforts of policy makers and cloud providers gathered behind The Green Grid consortium [8]. The problem with these metrics, though, is that they only focus on the infrastructure efficiency – turn as much energy as possible into computing inside the IT equipment. Once the power gets to the IT equipment, though, all formal energy efficiency regulation stops, making it more of a black-box approach. For this reason, an attempt is made in our work to bring energy efficiency control to the interior operation of clouds – resource scheduling.

So far, the measurement and control of even such a basic metric as PUE is not mandatory. It is considered a best practice, though, and agencies such as the U.S. Environmental Protection Agency (EPA) encourage data centers to measure it by rewarding the best data centers with the Energy Star award [2].

3   Applying the Kyoto Protocol to Clouds

The Kyoto protocol [19] commits involved countries to stabilize their greenhouse gas (GHG) emissions by adhering to the measures developed by the United Nations Framework Convention on Climate Change (UNFCCC) [12]. These measures are commonly known as *the cap-and-trade system*. It is based on setting national emission boundaries – caps, and establishing international emission markets for trading emission surpluses and emission deficits. This is known as *certified emission reductions* or *credits for emission reduction* (CERs). Such a trading system rewards countries which succeeded in reaching their goal with profits from selling CERs and forces those who did not to make up for it financially by buying CERs. The European Union Emission Trading System (EU ETS) is an example implementation of an emission trading market [4]. Through such markets, CERs converge towards a relatively constant market price, same as all the other tradable goods.

Individual countries control emissions among their own large polluters (individual companies such as power generation facilities, factories...) by distributing the available caps among them. In the current implementation, though, emission caps are only set for entities which are responsible for more than 25 $MtCO_2e$/year [3]. This excludes individual data centers which have a carbon footprint in the $ktCO_2e$/year range [1].

It is highly possible, though, that the Kyoto protocol will expand to smaller entities such as cloud providers to cover a larger percentage of polluters and to increase the chance of global improvement. One such reason is that currently energy producers take most of the weight of the protocol as they cannot pass the responsibilities on to their clients (some of which are quite large, such as data centers). In 2009, three companies in the EU ETS with the largest shortage of carbon allowances were electricity producers [5]. Another indicator of the justification of this forecast is that some cloud providers, such as Google already participate in emission trading markets to achieve carbon neutrality [7].

For this reason, we hypothesize in this paper that cloud providers are indeed part of an emission trading scheme and that CO_2e emissions have a market price.

4   Wastage-Penalty Balance in a Kyoto-Compliant Cloud

In this section we present our CO_2e-trading model that is to be integrated with cloud computing. We show how an economical balance can be found in it. Lastly, we give some discussion as to how such information might be integrated into a scheduler to make it more energy and cost efficient.

4.1   The CO_2e-Trading Model

The goal of our model is to integrate the Kyoto protocol's CO_2e trading mechanism with the existing cloud computing service-oriented paradigm. At the same time we want to use these two aspects of cloud computing to express an economical balance function that can help us make better decisions in the scheduling process.

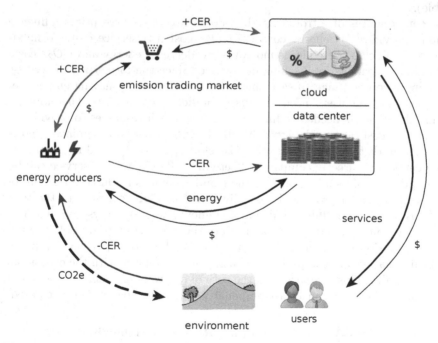

Fig. 1. Cloud computing integrated with the Kyoto protocol's emission trading scheme

The model diagram in Fig. 1 shows the entities in our model and their relations. A cloud offers some computing resources as services to its users and they in turn pay the cloud provider for these services. Now, a cloud is basically some software running on machines in a data center. To operate, a data center uses electrical energy that is bought from an energy producer. The energy producers are polluters as they emit CO_2e into the atmosphere. As previously explained, to mitigate this pollution, energy producers are bound by the Kyoto protocol to keep their CO_2e emissions bellow a certain threshold and buy CERs for all the excess emissions from other entities that did not reach their caps yet over the emission trading market (ETM). This is illustrated by getting negative CERs (-CERs) for CO_2e responsibilities and having to buy the same amount of positive CERs (+CERs) over the ETM. It does not make any real difference for our model if an entity reaches its cap or not, as it can sell the remaining CO_2e allowance as CERs to someone else over the ETM. Most importantly, this means that *CO_2e emissions an entity is responsible for have a price.*

The other important thing to state in our model is that *CO_2e emission responsibilities for the energy that was bought is transferred from the energy producer to the cloud provider.* This is shown in Fig. 1 by energy producers passing some amount of -CERs to the cloud provider along with the energy that was bought. The cloud provider then has to buy the same amount of +CERs via the ETM (or he will be able to sell them if he does not surpass his cap making them equally valuable).

The consequences of introducing this model are that three prices influence the cloud provider: (1) energy cost; (2) CO_2e cost; (3) service cost. To maximize profit, the cloud provider is motivated to decrease energy and CO_2e costs and maximize earnings from selling his service. Since the former is achieved by minimizing resource usage to save energy and the latter by having enough resources to satisfy the users' needs, they are conflicting constraints. Therefore, an economical balance is needed to find exactly how much resources to provide.

The service costs are much bigger than both of the other two combined (that is the current market state at least, otherwise cloud providers would not operate), so they cannot be directly compared. There are different ways a service can be delivered, though, depending on how the cloud schedules resources. The aim of a profit-seeking cloud provider is to deliver just enough resources to the user so that his needs are fullfilled and that the energy wastage stays minimal. If a user happens to be tricked out of too much of the resources initially sold to him, a service violation occurs and the cloud provider has to pay a penalty price. This means that we are comparing the energy wastage price with the occasional violation penalty. This comparison is the core of our wastage-penalty model and we will now explain how can a wastage-penalty economical balance be calculated.

4.2   The Wastage-Penalty Model for Resource Balancing

As was briefly sketched in the introduction, the main idea is to push cloud providers to follow their users' demands more closely, avoiding too much resource over-provisioning, thus saving energy. We do this by introducing additional cost factors that the cloud provider has to pay if he wastes too much resources – the energy and CO_2e costs shown in Fig. 1, encouraging him to breach the agreed service agreements and only provide what is actually needed. Of course, the cloud provider will not breach the agreement too much, as that could cause too many violation detections (by a user demanding what cannot be provided at the moment) and causing penalty costs. We will now expand our model with some formal definitions in the cloud-user interface from Fig. 1 to be able to explicitly express the wastage-penalty balance in it.

We assume a situation with one cloud provider and one cloud user. The cloud provides the user with a single, abstract resource that constitutes its service (it can be the amount of available data storage expressed in GB, for example). To provide a certain amount of this resource to the user in a unit of time, a proportional amount of energy is consumed and indirectly a proportional amount of CO_2e is emitted. An example resource scheduling scenario is shown in Fig. 2. An SLA was signed that binds the cloud provider to provide the user a constant resource amount, r_{agreed}. The cloud provider was paid for this service in advance. A user uses different resource amounts over time. At any moment the R_{demand} variable is the amount required by the user. To avoid over-provisioning the provider does not actually provision the promised resource amount all the time, but instead adapts this value dynamically, $r_{provisioned}$ is the resource amount allocated to the user in a time unit. This can be seen in Fig. 2 as $r_{provisioned}$ increases from t_1 to t_2 to adapt to a sudden rise in R_{demand}.

As we can not know how the user's demand changes over time, we will think of R_{demand} as a random variable. To express R_{demand} in an explicit way, some statistical method would be required and research of users' behaviour similar to that in [14] to gather real-life data regarding cloud computing resource demand. To stay on a high level of abstraction, though, we assume that it conforms to some statistical distribution and that we can calculate its mean $\overline{R}_{demand}$ and its maximum $max(R_{demand})$. To use this solution in the real world, an appropriate distribution should be input (or better yet – one of several possible distributions should be chosen at runtime that corresponds to the current user or application profile). We know the random variable's expected value E and variance V for typical statistical distributions and we can express $\overline{R}_{demand}$ as the expected value $E(R)$ and $max(R_{demand})$ as the sum of $E(R) + V(R)$ with a limited error.

Wastage Costs. Let us see how these variables can be used to model resource wastage costs. We denote the energy price to provision the whole r_{agreed} resource amount per time unit c_{en} and similarly the CO_2e price c_{co_2}. By only using the infrastructure to provision an amount that is estimated the user will require, not the whole amount, we save energy that would have otherwise been wasted and we denote this evaded wastage cost $c_{wastage}$. Since $c_{wastage}$ is a fraction of $c_{en} + c_{co_2}$, we can use a percentage w to state the percentage that is wasted:

$$c_{wastage} = w * (c_{en} + c_{co_2}) \qquad (1)$$

We know what the extreme cases for w should be – 0% for provisioning approximately what is needed, $\overline{R}_{demand}$; and the percentage equivalent to the ratio

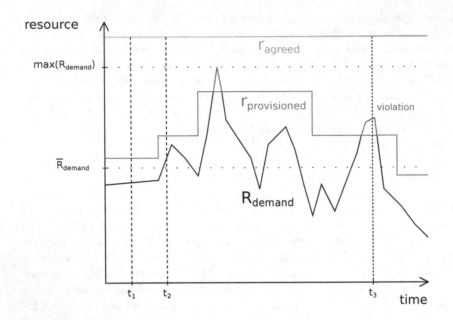

Fig. 2. Changes in the *provisioned* and *demand* resource amounts over time

of the distance between $\overline{R}_{demand}$ and r_{agreed} to the total amount r_{agreed} if we provision r_{agreed}:

$$w = \begin{cases} 1 - \dfrac{\overline{R}_{demand}}{r_{agreed}}, & \text{if } r_{provisioned} = r_{agreed} \\ 0, & \text{if } r_{provisioned} = \overline{R}_{demand} \end{cases} \tag{2}$$

We model the distribution of w between these extreme values using linear interpolation: average resource utilization - a ratio of the average provisioned resource amount ($\overline{r}_{provisioned}$) and the promised resource amount ($r_{promise}$):

$$w = \frac{r_{provisioned} - \overline{R}_{demand}}{r_{agreed}} \tag{3}$$

If we apply 3 to 1 we get an expression for the wastage cost.:

$$c_{wastage} = \frac{r_{provisioned} - \overline{R}_{demand}}{r_{agreed}} * (c_{en} + c_{co_2}) \tag{4}$$

Penalty Costs. Let us now use a similar approach to model penalty costs. If a user demands more resources than the provider has provisioned, an SLA violation occurs. The user gets only the provisioned amount of resources in this case and the provider has to pay the penalty cost C_{penal}. While c_{en} and c_{co_2} can be considered constant for our needs, C_{penal} is a random variable, because it depends on the user's behaviour which we can not predict with 100% accuracy, so we will be working with $E(C_{penal})$, its expected value.

$E(C_{penal})$, the expected value of C_{penal} can be calculated as:

$$E(C_{penal}) = p_{viol} * c_{viol} \qquad (5)$$

where c_{viol} is the constant cost of a single violation (although in reality probably not all kinds of violations would be priced the same) and p_{viol} is the probability of a violation occurring. This probability can be expressed as a function of $r_{provisioned}$, r_{agreed} and R_{demand}, the random variable representing the user's behaviour:

$$p_{viol} = f(\overline{r}_{provisioned}, r_{promise}, R_{demand}) \qquad (6)$$

Again, same as for $c_{wastage}$, we know the extreme values we want for p_{viol}. If 0 is provisioned, we have 100% violations and if $max(R_{demand})$ is provisioned, we have 0% violations:

$$p_{viol} = \begin{cases} 100\%, & \text{if } r_{provisioned} = 0 \\ 0\%, & \text{if } r_{provisioned} = max(R_{demand}) \end{cases} \qquad (7)$$

and if we assume a linear distribution in between we get an expression for the probability of violations occuring, which is needed for calculating the penalty costs:

$$p_{viol} = 1 - \frac{r_{provisioned}}{max(R_{demand})} \qquad (8)$$

Combining the Two. Now that we have identified the individual costs, we can state our goal function. If the cloud provider provisions too much resources the $c_{wastage}$ wastage cost is too high. If on the other hand he provisions too little resources, tightens the grip on the user too much, the $E(C_{penal})$ penalty cost will be too high. The economical balance occurs when the penalty and wastage costs are equal - it is profitable for the cloud provider to breach the SLA only up to the point where penalty costs exceed wastage savings. We can express this economical balance with the following equation:

$$c_{wastage} = E(C_{penal}) + [\text{customer satisfaction factor}] \qquad (9)$$

The [customer satisfaction factor] could be used to model how our promised-provisioned manipulations affect the user's happiness with the quality of service and would be dependant of the service cost (because it might influence if the user would be willing to pay for it again in the future). For simplicity's sake we will say that this factor equals 0, getting:

$$c_{wastage} = E(C_{penal}) \qquad (10)$$

Now, we can combine equations 4, 10, 5 and 8 to get a final expression for $r_{provisioned}$:

$$r_{provisioned} = \frac{max(R_{demand}) * \left[\overline{R}_{demand} * (c_{en} + c_{co_2}) + r_{agreed} * c_{viol}\right]}{max(R_{demand}) * (c_{en} + c_{co_2}) + r_{agreed} * c_{viol}} \qquad (11)$$

This formula is basically *the economical wastage-penalty balance*. All the parameters it depends on are constant as long as the demand statistic stays the same. It shows how much on average should a cloud provider breach the promised resource amounts when provisioning resources to users so that the statistically expected costs for SLA violation penalties do not surpass the gains from energy savings. Vice versa also holds – if a cloud provider provisions more resources than this wastage-penalty balance, he pays more for the energy wastage (energy and CO_2e price), than what he saves on SLA violations.

4.3 Heuristics for Scheduling Optimisation with Integrated Emission Management

In this section we discuss a possible application of our wastage-penalty model for the implementation of a future-generation data center. Knowing the economical wastage-penalty balance, heuristic functions can be used to optimize resource allocation to maximize the cloud provider's profit by integrating both service and violation penalty prices and energy and CO_2e costs. This is useful, because it helps in the decision-making process when there are so many contradicting costs and constraints involved.

A heuristic might state: "try not to provision more than $\pm x\%$ resources than the economical wastage-penalty balance". This heuristic could easily be integrated into existing scheduling algorithms, such as [21,20] so that the cloud provider does not stray too far away from the statistically profitable zone without deeper knowledge about resource demand profiles. The benefits of using our wastage-penalty model are:

- a new, expanded cost model covers all of the influences from Fig. 1
- CO_2e-trading schema-readiness makes it easier to take part in emission trading
- a Kyoto-compliant scheduler module can be adapted for use in resource scheduling and allocation solutions
- the model is valid even without Kyoto-compliance by setting the CO_2e price c_{co_2} to 0, meaning it can be used in traditional ways by weighing only the energy wastage costs against service violation penalties.

The wastage-penalty balance in 11 is a function of significant costs and the demand profile's statistical properties:

$$r_{provisioned} = g(max(R_{demand}), \overline{R}_{demand}, r_{agreed}, c_{en}, c_{co_2}, c_{viol}) \qquad (12)$$

This function enables the input of various statistical models for user or application demand profiles ($max(R_{demand})$ and $\overline{R}_{demand}$) and energy (c_{en}), CO_2e (c_{co_2}) and SLA violation market prices (c_{viol}). With different input parameters, output results such as energy savings, environmental impact and SLA violation frequency can be compared. This would allow cloud providers and governing decision-makers to simulate the effects of different scenarios and measure the influence of individual parameters, helping them choose the right strategy.

5   Conclusion

In this paper we presented a novel approach for Kyoto protocol-compliant modeling of data centers. We presented a conceptual model for CO_2e trading compliant with the Kyoto protocol's emission trading scheme. We consider an *emission trading market (ETM)* where CO_2e obligations are forwarded to data centers, involving them in the trade of credits for emission reduction (CERs). Such measures would ensure a CO_2e equilibrium and encourage more careful resource allocation inside data centers.

To aid decision making inside this CO_2e-trading system, we proposed a *wastage-penalty* model that can be used as a basis for the implementation of Kyoto protocol-compliant scheduling and pricing models. In the future we plan to implement prototype scheduling algorithms for the ETM considering self-adaptable Cloud infrastructures.

Acknowledgements. The work described in this paper was funded by the Vienna Science and Technology Fund (WWTF) through project ICT08-018 and by the TU Vienna funded HALEY project (Holistic Energy Efficient Management of Hybrid Clouds).

References

1. Data center energy efficiency calculator, http://www.42u.com/efficiency/energy-efficiency-calculator.html
2. ENERGY STAR data center energy efficiency initiatives : ENERGY STAR, http://www.energystar.gov/index.cfm?c=prod_development.server_efficiency
3. Environment agency - phase III 2013 to 2020, http://www.environment-agency.gov.uk/business/topics/pollution/113457.aspx#What_we_need_you_to_do_now
4. EU emissions trading system - department of energy and climate change, http://www.decc.gov.uk/en/content/cms/emissions/eu_ets/eu_ets.aspx
5. EU ETS 2009 company ratings, http://www.carbonmarketdata.com/cmd/publications/EU%20ETS%202009%20Company%20Rankings%20-%20June%202010.pdf
6. Gartner estimates ICT industry accounts for 2 percent of global CO2 emissions, http://www.gartner.com/it/page.jsp?id=503867

7. Google's PPAs: what, how and why, `http://static.googleusercontent.com/external_content/untrusted_dlcp/www.google.com/en/us/green/pdfs/renewable-energy.pdf`

8. The green grid, `http://www.thegreengrid.org/`

9. The green grid › CUEandWUE, `http://www.thegreengrid.org/Global/Content/TechnicalForumPresentation/2011TechForumCUEandWUE`

10. The green grid › the green grid metrics: Describing data center power efficiency, `http://www.thegreengrid.org/en/Global/Content/white-papers/Green-Grid-Metrics`

11. IPCC - intergovernmental panel on climate change, `http://www.ipcc.ch/publications_and_data/publications_ipcc_fourth_assessment_report_synthesis_report.html`

12. Kyoto protocol, `http://unfccc.int/kyoto_protocol/items/2830.php`

13. Kyoto protocol to the united nations framework convention on climate change, `http://unfccc.int/essential_background/kyoto_protocol/items/1678.php`

14. Beauvisage, T.: Computer usage in daily life. In: Proceedings of the 27th International Conference on Human Factors in Computing Systems, CHI 2009, pp. 575–584. ACM, New York (2009)

15. Beloglazov, A., Buyya, R.: Adaptive threshold-based approach for energy-efficient consolidation of virtual machines in cloud data centers. In: Proceedings of the 8th International Workshop on Middleware for Grids, Clouds and e-Science, MGC 2010, pp. pp. 4:1–4:6. ACM, New York (2010)

16. Coutinho, F., de Carvalho, L.A.V., Santana, R.: A workflow scheduling algorithm for optimizing Energy-Efficient grid resources usage. In: 2011 IEEE Ninth International Conference on Dependable, Autonomic and Secure Computing (DASC), pp. 642–649. IEEE (December 2011)

17. Ellerman, D., Joskow, P.: The european union's emissions trading system in perspective, prepared for the pew center on global climate change, `http://www.c2es.org/eu-ets`

18. Garg, S.K., Yeo, C.S., Anandasivam, A., Buyya, R.: Environment-conscious scheduling of HPC applications on distributed cloud-oriented data centers. Journal of Parallel and Distributed Computing 71(6), 732–749 (2011)

19. Grubb, M., Vrolijk, C., Brack, D.: Kyoto Protocol: A Guide and Assessment. Earthscan Ltd., London (1999)

20. Maurer, M., Brandic, I., Sakellariou, R.: Simulating Autonomic SLA Enactment in Clouds Using Case Based Reasoning. In: Di Nitto, E., Yahyapour, R. (eds.) ServiceWave 2010. LNCS, vol. 6481, pp. 25–36. Springer, Heidelberg (2010)

21. Maurer, M., Brandic, I., Sakellariou, R.: Enacting SLAs in Clouds Using Rules. In: Jeannot, E., Namyst, R., Roman, J. (eds.) Euro-Par 2011, Part I. LNCS, vol. 6852, pp. 455–466. Springer, Heidelberg (2011)

22. Wang, Z., Zhang, Y.: Energy-Efficient task scheduling algorithms with human intelligence based task shuffling and task relocation, pp. 38–43. IEEE (August 2011)

Implementation and Evaluation
of a Wired Data Center Sensor Network

Mikko Pervilä[1], Mikko Rantanen[1], and Jussi Kangasharju[2]

[1] University of Helsinki, Department of Computer Science
PL 68, 00014 Helsingin yliopisto, Finland
{pervila,mcrantan}@cs.helsinki.fi
[2] Helsinki Institute for Information Technology
Department of Computer Science
PL 68, 00014 Helsingin yliopisto, Finland
jakangas@cs.helsinki.fi

Abstract. As an alternative to often costly computational fluid dynamics (CFD) modelling of a data center (DC), we describe an ultra-low cost solution based on a wired sensor network. We describe the sensor hardware, packaging and cabling in detail, as well as the software components. Our prototype has been in production use for twelve months at the time of writing. This article presents detected air flow patterns that would have been difficult to discover using modelling alone, but easy to find with the measurement-based approach. We evaluate the benefits and drawbacks of our solution when compared with CFD models and existing alternatives. Key features of our approach are its accuracy, ease of deployment, and low purchase, construction, and operating costs.

1 Introduction

The benefit of building a CFD model is that proposed air flow modifications can be evaluated without the need of real changes in a DC. Yet CFD models are known to be both extremely computationally intensive and sensitive to any unanticipated air flow changes. The complexity required to calculate the complete air flow model is typically mitigated by simplifying the model, i.e., making generalizations about the conditions in the DC. The derived model is representative for a fixed point in time, but air flow changes can be caused by many day-to-day events in a DC, including hardware failures.

We argue that even though CFD can be useful in finding some problematic areas for air flow, without additional verification there can be no certainty that the CFD model remains precise for the whole DC. On the other hand, validating the entire CFD model for a large DC can be a serious burden. It is also difficult to describe the full complexity of a real DC in a model. Overlooked details can produce surprising defects in the resulting model, causing it to differ from the measured reality. The problem is the inherent requirement of true initial knowledge in a simulation-type study. For example, the effects of changes in the perforated floor tile configuration [13] and obstructions in the underfloor plenum [3] are well known.

J. Huusko et al. (Eds.): E²DC 2012, LNCS 7396, pp. 105–116, 2012.
© Springer-Verlag Berlin Heidelberg 2012

In CFD modelling, groups of servers are typically modelled as *blocks* with a homogeneous air flow. However, as new server designs are constantly produced, even units from a single vendor can have extremely varying airflow characteristics [12]. Devices like switches and routers can also eschew the front-to-back cooling pattern [10] completely. Server air flow is not proportional to the amount of power drawn by a server, is difficult to estimate based on reported fan speeds only, and can change considerably by reordering the same servers in the rack [10].

Even though CFD modelling might work well for newly built, homogeneous environments, it can fail in colocation-based data centers. In these DCs, the heterogeneity of the customer base leads to an equally diverse set of installed hardware. A similar type of evolution can be observed in warehouse-scale computing environments [8], after a subset of the initial equipment has been obsoleted or replaced due to failures.

In DCs reaching the warehouse-scale, failures become the norm, not an exception [1]. Even though air flow dynamics may change only a little when a single server is taken offline for repairs, failing power-distribution units (PDUs) or computer-room air conditioning (CRACs) units will have much more far-reaching consequences. During the past twelve months of operating our measurement system in our department's DC (see Sect. 3), we have encountered both a massive power supply failure and a CRAC failure. Knowing exactly where hot spots did and did not start to develop allowed our system administrators to avoid shutting down our computing equipment. Yet the time to react precluded a CFD-based approach, for the temperatures were rising by the hour.

The combined weight of these issues points to the fact that instead of CFD, measurement-based approaches have been revisited successfully in the past few years [2, 4–7, 11]. The contribution of this article is the complete description of an ultra-low cost *wired* sensor network which can be implemented in small- to medium-sized DCs within the order of days. As the sensors can be replaced with any equivalent devices, all the software components are open sourced, and the rest of the hardware is COTS equipment, the proposed solution is immediately available for all DC operators. Almost no skills in electronics are required, including soldering, and existing ethernet cabling may be reused. The sensor network can also be used to verify CFD models or act as a baseline for comparisons against more advanced, possibly wireless research experiments.

We present our implementation in Sect. 2. Section 3 presents some new discoveries, while Sect. 4 discusses the merits and flaws of our measurement-based solution. Section 5 concludes this article.

2   Design Decisions

By surveying the field of existing approaches it becomes clear that there are a number of vendors willing to sell or lease their measurement solutions, including advanced software applications designed for easy temperature visualization. On the other hand, a respected estimate [14] divides up to 72% of all DCs into the small- or closet-sized and medium categories. It follows that these smaller

DCs have smaller operating budgets, meaning that outsourced solutions can be prohibitively expensive.

Even though it is easy to agree that operating any DC in a manner which is "green" or "sustainable" is a desirable objective, the driving force behind business decisions still remains the purchase costs vs. benefits. Thus, our primary objectives have been to build a sensor network that is both cheap and very easy to install, yet so reliable it requires almost no manual upkeep. We will examine the latter two requirements first, then present our solution and calculate the actual costs for our implementation.

2.1 Wired versus Wireless

To our knowledge, the largest published number of operational temperature sensors is by HP [6, 4]. According to them, a 70,000 ft^2 (ca. 6,503 m^2) DC which employs 7,500 sensors has been operational since 2007 in Bangalore, India. This number translates to ca. 1.15 sensors/m^2, which we have considered a reasonable requirement. Unfortunately, nearly all of the other implementation details remain unknown. It is unlikely, however, that each sensor was cabled separately.

A number of previous solutions have concentrated on wireless or hybrid approaches in communicating with the temperature sensors. Microsoft Research's Genomotes [5] are implemented with a wireless master node which then daisy-chains up to seven slave nodes through the venerable RS-232 interface. The entire chain uses a single USB port for a power supply, although the master node also contains a rechargeable battery as a backup. Following Microsoft, chaining multiple sensors into a bus seemed reasonable.

Microsoft's justification for their hybrid approach is the ease of cabling since only the slave nodes need to be physically connected. The master nodes can reside at the top of the server racks and communicate wirelessly. They key problem of reliable wireless data collection is solved by Microsoft's RACNet solution. While we agree with their analysis of the overabundance of cabling already present in any modern DC, we differ in the conclusion. Since there is already so much cabling present, we consider that modest additions can still be tolerated. Thus, our solutions either adds its own or reuses existing, but unused cabling.

2.2 The Source of Power

Even if all of the data transfer can be performed wirelessly, present wireless technologies still require a separate power source for the sensors. On the other hand, replacing batteries can quickly become a tedious task for the DC operators. Thus, it would be prudent if a single wire can provide both a data signal and a power source. Fortunately, such products have been designed by multiple vendors, e.g., the Inter-Integrated Circuit (I^{2}C) by Philips and the 1-Wire by Maxim, formerly known as Dallas Semiconductors.

The idea in both product families is simple. By using from two to four conductors cabled together, a single cable can provide a network of devices both power and signals for a data channel. Such setups are particularly suitable for

Fig. 1. DS18B20 sensor packaged in a RJ11 female-female adapter

DC environments [7], because an unshielded twisted-pair cable will contain four
pairs equalling eight conductors. Moreover, the sensors use very robust signalling
techniques allowing reported cable lengths of up to 200 m. In our case, we chose
to use the existing ethernet cable rails, but connect our sensors using a separate
two-pair RJ11 cable in order to simplify our cabling design. All of our sensors
connect to a single bus presently.

2.3   Connecting the Sensors

We chose the 1-Wire products due to our previous experience with them, an open
source API, and good support from the Linux community. Auxiliary evidence
[4, 11] suggests that HP did employ sensors from the same manufacturer [7] in
their DCs around 2006. Our design is based on the Maxim DS18B20, which is
roughly a pin-sized[1] sensor with three conductor legs. It's accuracy is $\pm 0.5\,^{\circ}\mathrm{C}$
when operating in the range of $-10\,^{\circ}\mathrm{C}$ to $+85\,^{\circ}\mathrm{C}$. This sensor has remained in
production for a number of years, and is widely used by a large base of electronic
hobbyists and professionals alike.

In order to connect the DS18B20 to the RJ11 cable, we needed to package each
sensor for easy connectivity and eventual replacement when the sensor would fail.
Due to the cabling, the choice was easy, and we chose the RJ11 female-female
adapter jack used for cable extensions. To improve air flow, we used a drill press
to perforate the casing with four 4 mm holes. The jack itself can be easily pried

---

[1] http://www.maxim-ic.com/datasheet/index.mvp/id/2812

open into two halves, and with a little bit of gentle bending, the DS18B20 can be seated inside the plastic casing. Excluding the drill press, a single sensor can be built in three minutes or less with only minor practice. The end result is portrayed in Fig. 1 along a 1 € coin for size comparison.

The RJ11 jacks and cable form a sensor bus using 6-position, 4-conductor RJ11 connectors, and the bus itself terminates via a 6-position, 6-conductor RJ12 connector to a DS9490R adapter. The DS9490R is read through a host computer's USB port. Our current installation uses 15 sensors and over 75 m of cable. The limiting factor was that we simply did not need any more sensors. The sensor positioning is further explained in Sect. 3.

2.4 Results and Cost

Each DS9490R is read by the DigiTemp[2] Linux program, which scans for all sensors on the bus and then retrieves their temperature readouts. We wrote a very simple wrapper script to pipeline the data to the well-known RRDtool[3] utility. RRDtool is designed to redraw time series graphs in multiple formats and time resolutions (see Sect. 3). We poll all of our sensors every 60 seconds and archive copies of the DigiTemp outputs in addition to the RRDtool databases. RRDtool then graphs its data every five minutes and the graphs are copied to a publicly accessible directory[4].

We have published a full step-by-step instruction manual which includes detailed connection diagrams, photographs of each relevant step, and a video of the assembly process[5]. The total costs for our current solution amount to just under 160 € for the whole 15 sensor network, or more precisely, 10.51 € per sensor including taxes. These prices could be reduced by ordering the sensors directly from Maxim. While we paid 3.50 € per sensor, the quoted price is about $1.84 per sensor for orders of over 1,000 units. Also, for our modestly sized network, the USB host adapter price is almost half of the total.

3 Data and Knowledge

Our main DC has a floor space of just over $70\,m^2$ (ca. $750\,ft^2$). Despite the compact size, the DC draws over 115 kW of power during computationally heavy experiments. Cooling is handled by five CRAC units for the IT load plus one for the battery backup (not shown). The CRAC units are cooled by two separate chilling plants. Cool air from the CRAC units flows to an underfloor plenum and then through perforated tiles into the server inlets. All of the servers are placed into two rows with their fronts opposing each other, forming a cold aisle. The ends and roof of the aisle are sealed to prevent air recirculation, forming a cold

---

[2] http://www.digitemp.com/ by Brian C. Lane.
[3] http://oss.oetiker.ch/rrdtool/ by Tobias Oetiker.
[4] http://www.cs.helsinki.fi/group/greenict/
[5] http://blogs.helsinki.fi/pervila/?p=116

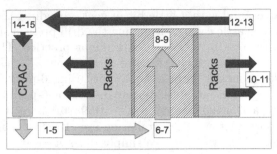

(a) Sensor placement, side view

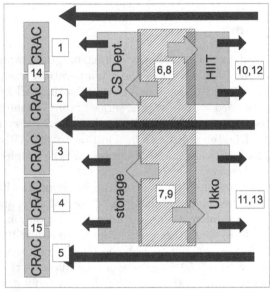

(b) Sensor placement, top view

Fig. 2. Sensor placement in the data center, side and top views

aisle containment (CAC) setup. The CAC is reasonably airtight. The CRACs form a third row on the west side of the cold aisle. For further details, see [9].

Figure 2 shows how we placed our 15 sensors. For each of the five CRAC units, we placed one sensor near their supply air vents in the underfloor plenum. Sensors 6–7 were placed just under the perforated floor tiles at 1/5 and 4/5 of the cold aisle length. Sensors 8–9 were placed at the corresponding lengths near the roof of the CAC section. Four sensors were placed at the same lengths on the exhaust or hot aisle side, near the opposite wall of the DC as seen from the CRACs. Sensors 10–11 were placed at 1 m height and 12–13 at 3 m height. Finally, sensors 14–15 were placed over the return vents of the CRAC units.

The placement logic is that we wish to measure the full cycle of the air flow from the CRAC units to the underfloor plenum, then upwards into the CAC section, out from the far side of the racks, over the top of the racks, and back into

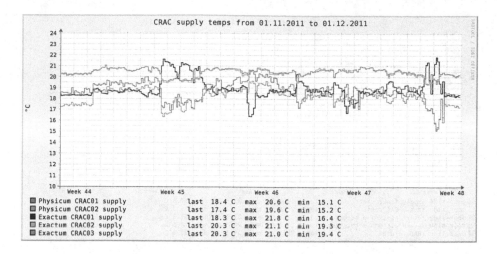

Fig. 3. CRAC supply temperatures from November 2011

the CRAC units. First, analyzing the graphs allows us to see whether the CRACs are supplying the DC with enough cooling. Second, we can detect increments in the supply air temperature from the CRAC units to the server inlets, caused by exhaust air recirculation. Third, temperature imbalances caused by different air flow requirements are visible by comparing sensor readouts from the lengthwise pairs. Finally, the exhaust measurements allow us to measure the heat removed by the CRACs, showing if heat is supplied or removed from the DC by other means.

3.1 Machines in Disagreement

Due to historical reasons, the five separate CRAC units are driven separately and not through a centralized system. In Fig. 3 we show the CRAC supply temperatures during November 2011. The two elder units, designated Physicum CRAC01 and CRAC02 in Fig. 3, make their cooling decisions based on a sensor located within the cold aisle. The three other units measure the ambient temperature locally and adjust their cooling power individually based on their measurements. Finally, the unit designated Exactum CRAC03 has been turned off. Thanks to the CAC, we have been able to save over a fifth of the required CRAC power [9].

The fluctuation of supply air temperature is not caused by the differing views of the CRACs alone. Figure 4 and Fig. 5 reveal differences in the return air temperatures, meaning that exhaust heat is divided unevenly across the row of four operating CRAC units. This is caused by the power supply cabling installed above the racks. The cables and connectors would be difficult to model using CFD, but show to be quite effective in restricting air flow. We will discuss other findings from Figures 4 and 5 in more detail below.

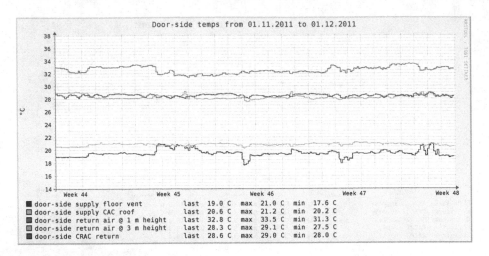

Fig. 4. Door-side temperatures from November 2011

The end result is that without a centralized management system, the four operational CRACs are continuously readjusting their blower speeds and supply air temperatures. Although all of the units have been manually tuned for a target supply temperature of 22° C, the max and min columns of Fig. 3 show that each unit fluctuates with varying variances. This effect has been previously reported by [2], and their centralized management system was able to save up to 58% of the CRAC operating power by minimizing the fluctuation.

3.2   Cold Aisle Imbalances

Figure 4 shows the top half of the DC shown in Fig. 2(b), designated as the *door-side*, following our IT administrators' naming convention. This half contains the even-numbered sensors 6–14. The other half is depicted in Fig. 5 and is designated the *rear-side*. It contains the odd-numbered sensors 7–15. In the figures, the lowest line shows the supply air temperature at the floor of the cold aisle and the second lowest line is the roof of the cold aisle. The top three lines (not clearly visible as three lines in Fig. 5) show the return air temperatures behind the racks (at heights of 1 and 3 m) and the CRAC return air temperature.

As the CRACs fluctuate, the two halves of the cold aisle receive different amounts of air flow and at different supply temperatures. The rear-side is supplied more by Physicum CRACs and consequently follows the target temperature of 22° C more precisely due to the better CRAC sensor placement. However, these CRACs end up performing the major part of the cooling, for warmer door-side supply air reaches the sensor, meddling with the CRACs decision logic.

Since our CAC is custom-built by ourselves, we have tried to ensure that it is relatively airtight near the key areas and blocks off exhaust air recirculation. Thus, Fig. 5 presents a very interesting question about the rise of the supply air

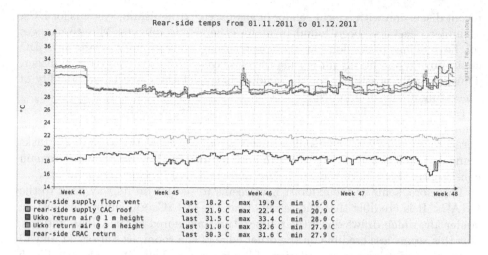

Fig. 5. Rear-side temperatures from November 2011

temperature from the bottom of the cold aisle to its roof. During normal operations, the delta is around 3° C, which can not be explained by heat conducted or radiated from within the cold aisle.

We have eliminated the possibility of a sensor failure and also verified that none of the installed servers or network devices are exhausting heat into the inlet side. Neither can the delta be satisfactorily explained by warmer supply air flowing from the other half of the cold aisle, as that half's supply temperature maximum just barely reaches this half's minimum. Thus, hot air seams to leak into the CAC from *somewhere else* than from within, the edges, or roof of the cold aisle.

After these options have been exhausted, not many possibilities remain. Our current hypothesis is that either a cold aisle underpressure or hot aisle overpressure is caused by the blade servers installed near the sensor. Either effect is then sufficient to push or draw exhaust air through or around the blade servers and into the cold aisle. We have been able to partially verify this hypothesis using a specially constructed server enclosure. By limiting either the inlet or the exhaust air flow, the inlet air temperatures do rise above the ambient temperature. In the enclosure, this heat must be derived from the exhaust air, since no other sources are nearby.

3.3   Not a Closed System

Although it is standard practice to model a DC as a closed system, this assumption does not seem to hold quite true in practice, although the difference is more difficult to detect. We have long suspected that the building where the DC is housed either contributes or burdens the cooling loads. According to a recent discussion with a local vendor of gas-based extinguishing systems for DCs, a similar effect has been found in many other environments. Minute changes to the building plans done at the construction site can cause drafts in a DC environment, potentially mitigating the effectiveness of a gas-based extinguisher. Thus, the only possibility for the vendors is to test the correct functionality of the extinguishers in practice.

Figure 4 shows that measured at the 1 m height, the exhaust air stays reasonably constant around 32° C, while Fig. 5 displays a much lower exhaust temperature around 29° C. The spikes in this graph are caused by computing tasks being executed at the blade servers. In both figures, the 1 m temperatures remain consistently above both the 3 m height and the CRAC return temperatures.

Therefore, some of the exhaust heat seems to be lost on its way back to the CRACs. It is credible that the servers near the CRACs are simply exhausting colder air, which draws down the temperatures measured at the CRAC returns. But this seems less credible on the other edge of the room, as sensors 11 and 13 measure a homogeneous installation of blade servers. Thus, it seems that Fig. 5 displays some of the heat being drawn by the building walls.

4   Discussion

In the previous section, we have demonstrated some events caught by our sensor network -based approach which would have been difficult to model without comparable initial knowledge about the DC installation. Our aim is not to prove CFD unfeasible, just to show that in some situations, the measurement-based approach can be a better starting point. The information gained from the measurement could then be used to build a much better model. In the case of small-to medium-sized DCs, the wired sensor network alone may suffice to discover the worst hotspots and subsequently optimize the cooling air flow.

4.1   Cost Evaluation

Perhaps the main merit of our implementation is its very affordable price. It is difficult to find comparable prices for a CFD-based approach. A single data point was presented during Google's European Data Summit 2011. During a retrofit of a network equipment DC the cost of "a couple of iterations" of CFD modelling was estimated as "USD\$5K–\$10K" (Joe Kava during his presentation[6]). As the actual load of the DC was around 85 kW and the maximum load around 250 kW, this gives us a possibility for a comparison.

Assuming the midpoint of the price range, the exchange rate of 0.761 € per dollar, and our actual price of 10.51 € per sensor we could purchase 914 sensors plus the required cables and accessories for connectivity. If our implementation generalizes to larger data centers, our density of 0.21 sensors/m² means that we can instrument a DC with a size of over 2,535 m². Even following HP's much

---

[6] http://www.youtube.com/watch?v=APynRrGuZJA around 11:17 / 27:52.

higher sensor density of 1.15 sensors/m^2 (see Sect. 2.1), the sensors could cover a DC of 471 m^2. As our price per sensor does not include workmanship costs, this comparison is not entirely fair. On the other hand, the quoted price range of \$5,000–\$10,000 very likely does not include software licenses.

4.2 Functionality and Reliability

The visualization software is definitely the weak point of the wired sensor-based approach. It is not difficult to discover that as a visualization engine RRDtool is quite old-fashioned in its syntax and hence, can be quite difficult to config-ure successfully. We are trying to mitigate these problems by releasing a set of helper scripts which make the initial steps much easier. In order to make the tem-perature information visually connect to the DC installation, some third party software is required to link the graphs near their correct locations on a map of the DC. One alternative for this is to use the NagVis[7] toolkit for the well-known Nagios[8] infrastructure monitoring daemon. As Nagios is very common in DC environments, this match seems natural and the solution straight-forward.

Compared with a wireless solution like Microsoft's Genomotes (see Sect. 2.1) the difference is that we have not fully solved the infrastructure problem. Each wired sensor bus must connect to a host computer, which must be able to run the DigiTemp application for sensor readouts. In addition, our solution does not come with a built-in battery backup. While these are true disadvantages to our approach, we feel that the prodigious cable lengths permitted by the sensor net-work mitigate the flaws at least somewhat. For a small- to medium-scale DC, not many sensor buses are really required. Similary, as the sensors themselves are ex-tremely Spartan in their energy consumption, a single backup battery could pro-vide enough power for the operation of both the sensors plus their host laptop.

5 Conclusion

In this article, we have provided the implementation details for a wired sensor network suitable for use in many small- and medium-scale data centers. As the proposed sensor network is both very inexpensive and fast to install, it can replace CFD-modelling in some DC installations, and thus work as a shortcut for system operators wishing to learn more about their DC's energy efficiency. In other installations, the sensor network could be used to gain initial insight before a full CFD modelling takes place, and verify the CFD model iteratively as it is being built. Finally, the proposed wired sensor network can be used as a baseline for comparing more advanced, possibly wireless sensor networks.

Through our own DC installation, we have evaluated some air flow conditions which would have been difficult to model without the measurement-based data. Our temperature graphs are available for interested parties, and we have also published a step-by-step guide describing in detail how to implement a similar sensor network.

---

[7] http://www.nagvis.org/screenshots
[8] http://www.nagios.org/

References

1. Barroso, L.A., Hölzle, U.: The Datacenter as a Computer: An Introduction to the Design of Warehouse-Scale Machines. Synthesis Lectures on Computer Architecture 4(1), 1–108 (2009)
2. Bash, C.E., Patel, C.D., Sharma, R.K.: Dynamic thermal management of air cooled data centers. In: The Tenth Intersociety Conference on Thermal and Thermomechanical Phenomena in Electronics Systems, ITHERM 2006, pp. 445–452. IEEE (2006)
3. Bhopte, S., Sammakia, B., Schmidt, R., Iyengar, M., Agonafer, D.: Effect of Under Floor Blockages on Data Center Performance. In: Proceedings of the 10th Intersociety Conference on Thermal and Thermomechanical Phenomena in Electronics Systems, ITHERM 2006, pp. 426–433 (2006)
4. Chen, K., Auslander, D.M., Bash, C.E., Patel, C.D.: Local Temperature Control in Data Center Cooling - Part I: Correlation Matrix. Tech. rep., HP Enterprise Software and Systems Laboratory, Palo Alto (2006), http://www.hpl.hp.com/techreports/2006/HPL-2006-42.pdf
5. Liu, J., Priyantha, B., Zhao, F., Liang, C., Wang, Q., James, S.: Towards discovering data center genome using sensor nets. In: Proceedings of the 5th Workshop on Embedded Networked Sensors, HotEmNets (2008)
6. Lowitt, E.M., Grimsley, J.: Hewlett-Packard: Sustainability as a Competitive Advantage (2009), http://www.hp.com/hpinfo/globalcitizenship/environment/commitment/accenturestudy.pdf
7. Mannas, E., Jones, S.: Add Thermal Monitoring to Reduce Data Center Energy Consumption (2009), http://www.maxim-ic.com/app-notes/index.mvp/id/4334
8. Mars, J., Tang, L., Hundt, R.: Heterogeneity in "Homogeneous" Warehouse-Scale Computers: A Performance Opportunity. IEEE Computer Architecture Letters 10(2), 29–32 (2011)
9. Pervilä, M., Kangasharju, J.: Cold air containment. In: Proceedings of the 2nd ACM SIGCOMM Workshop on Green Networking - GreenNets 2011, p. 7. ACM Press, New York (2011), http://dl.acm.org/citation.cfm?doid=2018536.2018539
10. Seymour, M., Aldham, C., Moezzi, H.: The Increasing Challenge of Data Center Design and Management: Is CFD a Must? (2011), http://www.electronics-cooling.com/issue/2011/11/
11. Vance, A.: HP fires data center robot, hires cooling sensors (2006), http://www.theregister.co.uk/2006/11/29/hp_cool/
12. VanGilder, J.W.: Real-Time Data Center Cooling Analysis (2011), http://www.electronics-cooling.com/2011/09/real-time-data-center-cooling-analysis/
13. VanGilder, J.W., Schmidt, R.R.: Airflow Uniformity Through Perforated Tiles in a Raised-Floor Data Center. In: Proceedings of IPACK 2005, pp. 493–501. ASME, San Francisco (2005)
14. Webb, M.: SMART 2020: Enabling the low carbon economy in the information age (2008), http://www.theclimategroup.org/publications/2008/6/19/smart2020-enabling-the-low-carbon-economy-in-the-information-age/

An Environmental Chargeback for Data Center and Cloud Computing Consumers

Edward Curry[1], Souleiman Hasan[1], Mark White[2], and Hugh Melvin[2]

[1] Digital Enterprise Research Institute (DERI),
IDA Business Park, Lower Dangan, Galway, Ireland
{ed.curry,souleiman.hasan}@deri.org
[2] Discipline of Information Technology, National University of Ireland, Galway,
University Road, Galway, Ireland
{m.white1,hugh.melvin}@nuigalway.ie

Abstract. Government, business, and the general public increasingly agree that the polluter should pay. Carbon dioxide and environmental damage are considered viable chargeable commodities. The net effect of this for data center and cloud computing operators is that they should look to "chargeback" the environmental impacts of their services to the consuming end-users. An environmental chargeback model can have a positive effect on environmental impacts by linking consumers to the indirect impacts of their usage, facilitating clearer understanding of the impact of their actions. In this paper we motivate the need for environmental chargeback mechanisms. The environmental chargeback model is described including requirements, methodology for definition, and environmental impact allocation strategies. The paper details a proof-of-concept within an operational data center together with discussion on experiences gained and future research directions.

Keywords: Sustainability, Chargeback Model, Data Center, Energy Efficiency, Cloud Computing.

1 Introduction

Google estimates that to answer a single search requires 0.0003kWh of energy and generates the equivalent of about 0.2g of CO_2. A 1-minute YouTube stream requires 0.0002kWh of energy and generates approximately 0.1g of CO_2. A single Gmail user requires 2.2kWh every year, and generates 1.2kg of CO_2. In 2010 Google's total carbon footprint was 1.46 million metric tons of CO_2[1]. However, is Google solely responsible for these emissions or do the 1 billion users that consume Google's services bear some responsibility? Do these users bear the responsibility equally (1.46 billion kg CO_2/1 billion users = 1.46 kg of CO2 per user per year) or do some power

---

[1] All figures published by Google at http://www.google.com/green/bigpicture/ retrieved on 23rd April 2012. Figure are for data-center emissions only and do not include end-user footprint.

J. Huusko et al. (Eds.): E²DC 2012, LNCS 7396, pp. 117–128, 2012.
© Springer-Verlag Berlin Heidelberg 2012

users cause more emissions than occasional light users? Are the users aware of the environmental effects of their usage? Should consumers of data center-based cloud services be accountable for the emissions associated with their service usage?

Government, business, and the general public increasingly agree that the polluter should pay. Carbon dioxide and environmental damage are considered viable chargeable commodities. The net effect for data center and cloud computing operators is that they should look to *"chargeback"* the environmental impacts, in addition to the financial costs, of their services to the consuming end-users.

Chargebacks can have a positive effect on environmental impacts by linking consumers to the indirect impacts of their service usage, allowing them to understand the impact of their actions. In this paper we motivate the need for environmental chargeback mechanisms to inform consumers of their data center environmental impacts.

The rest of this paper is organized as follows: Section 2 discusses the need for environmental chargeback for data center consumers. The environmental chargeback model is introduced in section 3 with discussion on the requirements, a methodology for defining chargeback models, and environmental impact allocation. A proof-of-concept implementation of the model within an operational data center is presented in section 4. Section 5 outlines related work and section 6 concludes with proposals for future research directions.

2   The Need for an Environmental Chargeback for Consumers

In this section we examine the environmental impact of data centers and cloud computing. For the sake of brevity, discussion on environmental impacts is limited to impacts associated with electricity generation in the operational phase of a data center. The authors note that power consumption does not tell the full story of the impacts of data centers on the environment[2]. However, we believe the approach purposed in this paper has the potential to be applied beyond power to include other impacts such as water, construction materials, facilities equipment, and IT equipment.

2.1   Data Centers and Cloud Computing Energy Impact Analysis

As corporate and home users move their IT services to the cloud, the growth of data center-based services is set to continue. Power consumption largely defines a data center's environmental impact: The amount of power that a data center uses on a day-to-day basis determines how much irreplaceable fossil fuels it consumes and the

---

[2] In order to understand the full environmental burden a full Life Cycle Assessment (LCA) of the data center facilities and IT equipment is needed. Take for example Microsoft's data center in Quincy, Washington that consumes 48 megawatts (enough power for 40,000 homes) of power. In addition to the concrete and steel used in the construction of the building the data center uses 4.8km of chillers piping, 965km of electrical wire, $92,900m^2$ of drywall, and 1.5 metric tons of batteries for backup power. Each of these components has their own impact that must be analysed in detail.

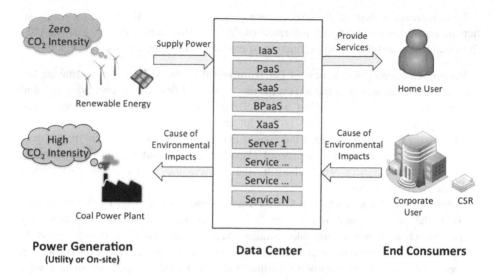

Fig. 1. Data Center Service Supply Chain

quantity of carbon emissions for which it is responsible. In 2010 the total electricity use by data centers was estimated between 1.1% and 1.5% of all electricity use for the world. For the US, that number was between 1.7% and 2.2% [1].

Within the supply chain of data center services, illustrated in Figure 1, the main emission occurs at the power generation site. Location is a key factor for the CO_2 intensity of the power consumed by the data center. A gas or coal fired power utility creates much more CO_2 than a hydro- or wind-power utility. For this reason, many new data centers (e.g. Google's) are located near low-cost and environmentally friendly power sources.

Data centers generate heat and must be cooled; the required equipment can be a significant consumer of power. Geographic location is also a key factor in cooling; a data center in a cool climate such as Ireland requires less cooling power than a data center in a warmer climate such as Mexico.

Based on these factors (and many others) the resulting CO_2 footprint of a data center can vary significantly, thus the execution of similar workloads in two different data centers can also vary.

2.2   Empowering the Consumer with Environmental Information

The principle of *'the polluter pays'* is gaining widespread acceptance among governments, business, and the general public. The end-users of data center services and their needs for IT services are the ultimate reason for the existence of the data center. However, very little information flows to the service consumer about the environmental impacts associated with their service execution. The result is that consumers are not well informed of the environmental consequences of their service usage, and thus have little opportunity to change their behavior to be more ecologically sound.

The challenge is how to tie environmental impacts back to the point of usage, so that the consumer can be better informed of their contribution to data center activity. The objective is to promote the reduction of environmental impacts by:

- **Raising Consumer Awareness of Environmental Impacts:** Improving sustainability performance requires information on the use, flows and destinies of energy, water, and materials including waste, along with monetary information on environment-related costs, earnings, and savings. This type of information is critical if we are to understand the causal relationships between the various actions that can be taken, and their impact on sustainable performance. Increased clarification will lead to consumers making more informed choices when choosing the services they use and the data centers providing those services.
- **Induce Efficient Usage of Data Center-Based Resources:** Consumers are concerned about the environmental impacts of their actions and will make environmentally friendly choices where possible. Studies have shown that improving access to information on consumption can reduce the overall usage of a resource (i.e. paper [2], energy [3][4]). It is reasonable to assume that if appropriate usage information were available for data center services, it would reduce usage. Empowering end-users to make sustainable choices requires them to know the environmental impacts of their action at the point of consumption, so they can make informed choices. Could the service be scheduled (invoked) when more renewable power sources are available? Could it be invoked less often?
- **Embed Service Usage within Sustainable IT Practices:** Corporate IT departments concerned with sustainability may have a sustainable IT program with the objective of reducing the environmental footprint of IT [5]. A chargeback would allow environmental impacts of IT service usage to be embedded within business and decision-making processes. It would enable IT departments to consider environmental impacts within the full life-cycle [6] of their cloud computing strategies.

3   An Environmental Chargeback Model for Consumers

Carbon dioxide and environmental damage are becoming more accepted as chargeable commodities. Determining how much environmental impact is being caused by an service end-user within a data center would make it possible to levy charges based on the impacts occurred, thus linking consumer activity with the environmental cost of the IT supporting it.

Pay for Use has long been a cornerstone of many business models (i.e. telephony, water, & waste). Pay for use models can increase awareness of the costs of resource usage and promote more efficient and selective usage, resulting in less waste and lower costs. To this end we purpose the use of a pay for use "chargeback" model for environmental impacts associated with data center services and cloud computing.

The purpose of the chargeback model is to allocate the environmental impacts of providing data center services to the service consumers: that is, making the consumer accountable for the environmental impacts of their service usage. Developing a chargeback model with billing based on actual resource usage, instead of resource allocation or reservation, is a fundamental requirement to encourage users to have more sustainable behaviors. An effective chargeback model should have the following benefits:

- Correlate service utilization with service consumers or corporate departments.
- Provide visibility into service and associated resource utilization.
- Enable consumers to understand their data center environmental footprint.
- Add transparency to sustainability of outsourced enterprise IT.
- Encourage the use of green power with lower environmental footprint.

3.1   Model Requirements

A chargeback model should meet the following requirements:

- **Equitable:** The consumer is only charged for the impacts they cause. One consumer should not subsidize the impacts of another consumer.
- **Accurate & Auditable:** Charge for actual impacts accurately and fully, and maintain records to handle inquiries and disputes.
- **Understandable:** Charging process & methodology must be comprehensible to consumers.
- **Controllable & Predictable:** Consumers must have the ability to control or predict the cost of performing a particular activity.
- **Flexible & Adaptable:** Ability to handle multiple service types (i.e. PaaS, IaaS, SaaS) and dynamic cost models (i.e. include capital impacts, operational impacts, and intermittent availability of renewables that can vary over time or by region).
- **Scalable:** Can handle small- and large-scale services.
- **Economical:** The model itself must be relatively inexpensive to design, implement, deploy, and run, including data collection, processing, and reporting to consumers.

3.2   Model Definition Methodology

We propose the following methodology to define environmental chargeback models:

Step 1. Identify service and define environmental system boundary: Identify the target service. Define the system boundary for environmental impacts of the model. Determine what type of information is needed to inform consumers and decision makers. Define the functional units that will be used (environmental impacts, energy efficiency, life span, cost per use, etc.).

Step 2. Identify the billable items and, for each one, identify the smallest unit available as a service to consumers: The goal of this step is to find a unit of measurement that makes it easy to aggregate and store billing data. The unit should also be an easily understood *charging unit* to the consumer.

- *Billable Service Items:* Resources for which consumers will be charged. These will be part of the IT service catalog, and consumers will be able to purchase these items. Examples of billable service items include, servers, virtual machines, storage, email, search, etc.

- *Atomic Service Units:* The smallest possible unit of measurement and collection, for a billable item, that will be used for billing purposes. The consumer bill will typically contain information on how many atomic units of a resource were used.

Step 3. Identify, analyze, and document relevant environmental impacts: Determine service resource use and associated environmental impacts. The data must be related to the functional unit defined in Step 1 and includes all data related to environmental impacts (e.g. CO_2) within the system boundaries.

Step 4. Define an environmental cost allocation strategy for each billable service item: After the environmental impacts have been identified, the billable service items have been identified, and the atomic service units have been defined, it is possible to build one or more environmental cost allocation strategies. Building an allocation strategy requires associating impacts to billable service items that are offered to service consumers. Each billable service item can have different allocation method that can use fixed, variable, or mixed charging. In order to maximize the benefits from cost allocation, it is necessary for allocation to reflect actual usage.

Step 5. Identify, integrate, and deploy the tools necessary to collect data and to calculate the environmental chargeback: A chargeback model implementation, illustrated in Figure 2, will typically require environmental data collection, DC resource utilization, service workload, chargeback calculation, and billing & reporting. The collection tools will vary based on the service and the data center.

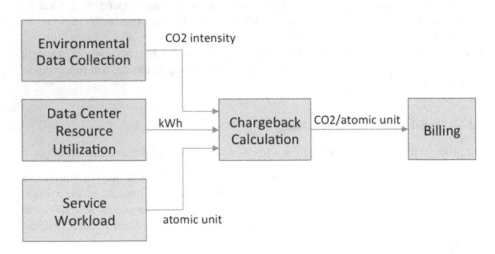

Fig. 2. Information workflow within environmental chargeback model

3.3   Allocating Environmental Impacts

To be able to determine the correct environmental impact allocation strategy it is necessary to know the direct and indirect costs of providing data center services. Similar to financial costs, environmental costs can be broken into Capital (initial/setup) or Operational (ongoing/running).

- **Capital Impacts** include the impacts of building the data center facilities and the impacts of the associated IT (server, network, storage, racks, cabling, etc.) and facilities equipment (i.e. power and cooling infrastructure). For capital items, the impact needs to be amortized over the life of the item. Typically servers have a lifespan of 3 to 5 years, while data center facilities have a lifespan of 10 to 15 years. Capital impacts may also extend to software artifacts. For example, the cost of building a search index may be orders of magnitude more expensive than the costs of user searches against the index. Software artifacts could have a useful lifespan in days, week, or months. A chargeback model should reflect these costs in a fixed charge over the estimated useful life of the equipment/software.
- **Operational Impacts** include all environmental impacts for keeping the data center running. The primary operational impact is power generation and water for cooling. Operational impacts are more straightforward to allocate and can usually be allocated by usage, such as the energy costs of running a server.

Both of these types of impacts must be taken into account within a chargeback model. It is important to be pragmatic with respect to the complexity of the chargeback model and the environmental data available. Setting a realistic environmental system boundary for the chargeback is essential to keeping its implementation straightforward.

4   Proof of Concept Implementation

In order to validate the proposed approach for the chargeback model a proof of concept (PoC) has been realized for a service within the DERI data center. In this section we discuss how the PoC chargeback model was defined, and how the resulting information is presented to the consumer. The section ends with a discussion on insights gained from the PoC.

4.1   Model Definition

The chargeback model in the PoC was defined as:

Step 1: The target is a transaction-based data service. The environmental system boundary of the model will be the carbon dioxide emissions associated with power generation. The chargeback model will be applied to the carbon emissions that are produced as a result of using the data service. The functional units are CO_2 in grams (gCO_2), kilowatts (kW) and kilowatt-hours (kWh).

Step 2: *Billable Service Items:* User accounts for the data service. *Atomic Service Units:* Single data transaction executed on the service.

Step 3. The chargeback model was scoped to cover the emissions associated with power generation. The data service runs on 27 dedicated servers[3], and the power supplied is from a mixture of fossil fuel power plants, and renewable energy sources (primarily wind). This results in a varying CO_2 intensity of the power based on the availability of renewable energy.

Step 4. Within the data service the computational workload of all transactions is similar, thus the energy cost between transactions is similar. This enabled us to treat transactions as equal from an impact allocation perspective. To quantify a single transaction we need to know 1) the energy consumed by the total service, 2) the CO_2 emissions of the energy, and 3) the total number of transactions. In order to establish this in real-time we utilize a sliding window-based calculation[4]. During the sliding-window the following data is gathered: *Total Service Energy*, *Number of Transactions Served*, and *CO_2 Intensity of Power Supply*. Impacts are allocated to the atomic service units according to the formula in equation 1.

$$CO_2 \text{ per Transaction} = \frac{\text{Total Service Energy} \times CO_2 \text{ Intensity}}{\text{Number of Transactions}} \tag{1}$$

Step 5. The implementation of the model leverages a number of existing monitoring infrastructures within the data center. These systems have been integrated together to deliver the chargeback model. The major sub-systems of the implementation are:

- **Real-Time Web Service for Power CO_2 Intensity**[5] based on the energy source mix (renewables, gas, oil.) that is used by power utilities in Ireland.
- **Data Center Resource Energy Monitor:** Provides data on the power consumption of the data center hardware used by the data service. Power distribution units in the datacenter are equipped with electricity metering capability.
- **Data Service Workload Monitor:** Provides data on user workload of the service.
- **Chargeback Calculation:** The chargeback model is encoded as rules within a Complex Event Processing (CEP) [7] engine. The CEP engine constantly receives events from each of the above systems, allocates impacts in real-time, then forwards the charge to the billing system. Data interoperability between existing infrastructures is achieved within the Linked dataspace for Energy Intelligence (LEI).
- **Billing System:** Provides reporting on charges to consumers.

4.2   Chargeback in Action

Figure 3 illustrates a screenshot showing actual chargeback results from the PoC. This interface provides the service consumer with an overview of their service usage, together with information on the current cost of a service invocation. As the CO_2

---

[3] Network and data storage devices were excluded due to insufficient metering.
[4] A limitation of this approach is that it ignores transactions that may have been initiated prior to the start of the window and those that do not complete prior to the end of the window.
[5] The Energy Research Center at UCD provides this service http://erc.ucd.ie/realtimedata/

intensity varies with the proportion of renewable energy that is used for power generation, consumers are be notified of the current proportion of renewables and forecasts for the predicted future availability. This can enable them to plan for greener use of the service. The interface details:

- Consumer Service Usage
  - Data transactions: Total number of transactions during billing period.
  - Cost per transaction: Average gCO_2 caused by single transaction during billing period.
- Current Service Cost
  - Current Cost of transaction in Wh, and a mean cost over the last 5 seconds.
  - Latest fuel mix for power generation.
  - Current cost of transaction in gCO_2.
- IT Infrastructure
  - Number of machines involved in service execution.
  - Total average acclimated power per machine during billing period.

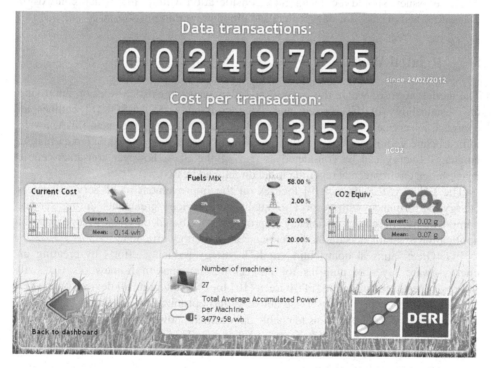

Fig. 3. Chargeback results from DERI Energy

4.3   Experiences and Discussion

In the process of implementing the PoC, we gained a number of insights into chargeback models.

- **Metering and Monitoring:** The PoC piggy-backed on existing billing/monitoring infrastructure for the services. Where such infrastructure is already in place, the model implementation can be simplified by reusing it. Service-level monitoring will need to match the atomic service units identified. Where this is not available the service-monitoring infrastructure may need to be extended to support it.
- **Service & Infrastructure Complexity:** Defining the allocation strategy is dependent on the complexity of the service interaction model, the supporting IT infrastructure, and resource variation between atomic service units. The PoC had a straightforward IT deployment and atomic service units. However, if a service is delivered by complex infrastructure, that is shared and federated across multiple data centers, the implementation of the cost allocation mode will be more difficult.
- **Stakeholder Collaboration:** Co-operation between facilities and IT in the data center has been a challenge within the industry. Deploying chargeback models will require collaboration from more players, such as service managers and developers.
- **Security and Privacy:** While not a direct focus of this work, the authors acknowledge that security and privacy concerns can arise with chargeback models. These issues should be taken into consideration within the wider context of security and privacy for data centers and cloud computing.

5   Related Work

The model proposed within this paper is complementary to existing work on improving the sustainability of data centers and cloud computing. SLA@SOI [8] outlines an approach to service management by embedding Service-Level Agreement (SLA) aware infrastructure within services. It defines assessment criteria using a custom representation language. Energy can be considered as part of the SLA, however consumer-centric usage-based environmental reporting is not directly addressed.

The EU GAMES project [9] focuses on the improvement of IT service centers energy performance with respect to quality of service agreements during service composition. The energy efficiency improvement is based on a knowledge base of application level impacts on the IT service centers energy efficiency.

FIT4Green aims at contributing to ICT energy reducing efforts by creating an energy-aware layer of plug-ins for data center automation frameworks that will improve energy consumption. FIT4Green [10] looks to integrate all devices connected (including networking) with service delivery into optimization policies. ALL4Green, a follow-on to FIT4Green, aims to enable data centers, power suppliers, and end-users to communicate their expected supply and demand. This will allow ICT resources to be better allocated to provide requested services, while saving energy and reducing greenhouse gas (GHG) emissions.

5.1   Data Center Energy Efficiency Metrics

When assessing the financial health of a business, one should not look at one metric in isolation. The same is true for assessing the efficiency of a data center. In this section we will examine a number of key metrics defined by the Green Grid to understand the sustainability of a data center[6].

Power Usage Effectiveness (PUE) is a measure of how efficiently a data center uses its power. PUE measures how much power the computing equipment consumes in contrast to cooling and other overheads. The reciprocal of PUE is *Data Center infrastructure Efficiency (DCiE)*. Both PUE and DCiE metrics give an indication as to the use of power by supporting infrastructure of the data center. Ideally PUE would equal one, meaning no additional energy is consumed to support the IT load.

Water Usage Effectiveness (WUE) measures data center water usage to provide an assessment of the water used on-site for operation of the data center. This includes water used for humidification and water evaporated on-site for energy production or cooling of the data center and its support system. *Carbon Usage Effectiveness (CUE)* measures data center-level carbon emissions. CUE does not cover the emissions associated with the lifecycle of the equipment in the data center or the building itself.

The Data Center Productivity (DCP) framework is a collection of metrics that measure the consumption of a data center-related resource in terms of data center output. DCP looks to define what a data center accomplishes relative to what it consumes. *Data Center compute Efficiency (DCcE)* enables data center operators to determine the efficiency of compute resources. The metric makes it easier for data center operators to discover unused servers (both physical and virtual) and decommission or redeploy them.

All the above metrics focus on data center efficiency to help data center operators identify opportunities for efficiency improvements. While these metrics can inform the consumer that they are using an efficient data center, they do not inform the consumer of the cost of their service usage. They do not give consumers the information necessary to improve the sustainability of their behavior.

6   Conclusions and Future Work

In this paper we have motivated the need to link data center service and cloud consumers with the impacts of their service usage, allowing them to understand the environmental consequences of their actions. We proposed the need for environmental chargeback models including discussion on their requirements, definition methodology, and environmental impact allocation. A proof-of-concept implementation of the model within an operational data center is described together with experienced gained.

Future research directions will focus on a user evaluation to determine if chargeback models can effectively change user behavior and reduce the impact of services. For example, will users choose to use the service when more renewable energy is available, meaning less CO_2 emissions? Other avenues of investigation include challenges associated with deploying chargeback models within different data

---

[6] White papers detailing all Green Grid metrics are available at
http://www.thegreengrid.org

center environments (i.e. homogenous & heterogeneous), at large scale (i.e. warehouse size), and appropriate strategies for the allocation of capital environmental impacts.

Acknowledgements. We would like to acknowledge the constructive comments of reviewers. The work presented in this paper is funded by Science Foundation Ireland under Grant No. SFI/08/CE/I1380 (Lion- 2).

References

1. Koomey, J.: Growth in Data center electricity use 2005 to 2010. Analytics Press, Oakland (2011)
2. Medland, R.C.: Curbing paper wastage using flavoured feedback. In: Proceedings of OZCHI 2010 Design–Interaction–Participation, pp. 22–26. Association for Computing Machinery (ACM) Press (2010)
3. Abrahamse, W., Steg, L., Vlek, C., Rothengatter, T.: A review of intervention studies aimed at household energy conservation. Journal of Environmental Psychology 25, 273–291 (2005)
4. Darby, S.: The effectiveness of feedback on energy consumption. A review for DEFRA of the literature on metering, billing and direct displays. Environmental Change Institute University of Oxford 22, 1–21 (2006)
5. Donnellan, B., Sheridan, C., Curry, E.: A Capability Maturity Framework for Sustainable Information and Communication Technology. IEEE IT Professional 13, 33–40 (2011)
6. Conway, G., Curry, E.: Managing Cloud Computing: A Life Cycle Approach. In: 2nd International Conference on Cloud Computing and Services Science (CLOSER 2012), Porto, pp. 198–207 (2012)
7. Hasan, S., Curry, E., Banduk, M., O'Riain, S.: Toward Situation Awareness for the Semantic Sensor Web: Complex Event Processing with Dynamic Linked Data Enrichment. In: 4th International Workshop on Semantic Sensor Networks 2011 (SSN 2011), Bonn, Germany, pp. 69–81 (2011)
8. Wieder, P., Butler, J.M., Theilmann, W., Yahyapour, R. (eds.): Service Level Agreements for Cloud Computing. Springer, Heidelberg (2011)
9. Bertoncini, M., Pernici, B., Salomie, I., Wesner, S.: GAMES: Green Active Management of Energy in IT Service Centres. In: Soffer, P., Proper, E. (eds.) CAiSE Forum 2010. LNBIP, vol. 72, pp. 238–252. Springer, Heidelberg (2011)
10. Basmadjian, R., Bunse, C., Georgiadou, V., Giuliani, G., Klingert, S., Lovasz, G., Majanen, M.: FIT4Green - Energy aware ICT Optimization Policies. In: COST Action IC0804 on Energy Efficiency in Large Scale Distributed Systems - 1st Year (2010)

Energy Usage and Carbon Emission Optimization Mechanism for Federated Data Centers

Dang Minh Quan[1], Andrey Somov[2], and Corentin Dupont[2]

[1] Institute of Information Technology for Economic,
National Economic University, Vietnam
quandm@upb.de
[2] CREATE-NET, Trento, Italy
{asomov,cdupont}@create-net.org

Abstract. This work addresses the problem of high energy consumption and carbon emissions by data centers which support the *traditional* computing style. In order to overcome this problem we consider two allocation scenarios: *single allocation* and *global optimization* of available resources and propose the optimization algorithms. The main idea of these algorithms is to find a server in the data center with the lowest energy consumption and/or carbon emission based on current status of data center and service level agreement requirements, and move the workload there. The optimization algorithms are devised based on Power Usage Effectiveness (PUE) and Carbon Usage Effectiveness (CUE). The simulation results demonstrate that the proposed algorithms enable the saving in energy consumption from 10% to 31% and in carbon emission from 10% to 87%.

Keywords: data center, traditional computing, power consumption, green computing, resource management.

1 Introduction

Until recently, the key performance indicator of a data center was its performance. However, the growing number of IT services and large scale tasks, resulting in higher power consumption [1] and carbon emission, have forced the ICT community to concern the energy efficiency of data centers carefully [2].

Several energy-aware approaches and resource management techniques have been introduced to tackle power consumption problem in the data center domain from different points of view. Many approaches are focused on workload consolidation in order to decrease the number of servers by switching them off/sleep and, therefore, to reduce the power consumption [3] [4]. Some techniques, in contrast, put efforts in finding the solutions of optimal workload placement in order to minimize the cooling systems energy consumption [5] while similar research works investigate the opportunity to reduce the power consumption of cooling systems by using intelligent scheduling or choosing the optimum temperature of cold air [7] [8]. The biological algorithm in [6] determines more power efficient servers within a data center facility and moves workload there.

J. Huusko et al. (Eds.): E²DC 2012, LNCS 7396, pp. 129–140, 2012.

The objective of this research work is twofold: to reduce the *power consumption* and *carbon emission* of a federated data center with the traditional mode of computation. To achieve this objective we propose the optimization algorithms for the single allocation of virtual machines and for global resources optimization.

The paper is organized as follows: Section 2 describes the problem formulation. Sections 3 and 4 present the algorithm for single allocation request and global optimization respectively. The simulation results based on different scenarios and the data centers configurations are shown in Section 5. Finally, we conclude and discuss our future work in Section 6.

2   Problem Formulation

We assume that we have a set of data centers D including N centers. Assume that in each data center d_l we have a set of servers S_l. Each server $s_{li} \in S_l$ is characterized with the number of cores and the amount of memory ($s_{li} \cdot nr\_Core$ and $s_{li} \cdot nr\_RAM$, respectively). As servers use central storage infrastructures (such as SAN, NAS or iSCSI external storage arrays), we do not have to care about storage in each server.

Each server s_{li} has a set of running virtual machines V_{li} including k_{li} virtual machines. Each virtual machine $v_j \in V_{li}$ is characterized with required number of virtual CPU and amount of memory ($v_j \cdot r\_vCPU$ and $v_j \cdot r\_RAM$, respectively) and the average CPU usage rate computed in % and the amount of memory ($v_j \cdot a\_Urate$, $v_j \cdot a\_RAM$).

With each server s_{li} the following constraints (1)-(4) have to be met. The total usage rate of a certain number of CPUs on a certain number of VMs can not exceed the safe performance factor for this certain number of cores:

$$\sum_{j=1}^{k_{li}} v_j \cdot r\_vCPU * v_j \cdot a\_Urate <= k * s_{li} \cdot nr\_Core \tag{1}$$

where k is the safe performance factor, $k < 1$.

The average total memory used by the VMs on one server cannot exceed the amount of total available memory of the server:

$$\sum_{j=1}^{k_{li}} v_j \cdot a\_RAM <= s_{li} \cdot nr\_RAM \tag{2}$$

The total number of VMs with required number of virtual CPUs is less or equal to number of cores with predefined maximum number of virtual CPUs on board:

$$\sum_{j=1}^{k_{li}} v_j \cdot r\_vCPU <= s_{li} \cdot nr\_Core * \max vCPUpCore \tag{3}$$

where *maxvCPUpCore* is maximum number of virtual CPUs per Core.

The number of the server's VMs can not exceed the maximum number of VMs, *maxVMpServer*, allowed for the server:

$$k_{li} <= \max VMpServer \tag{4}$$

2.1   Allocation Request

Assume we assign a new virtual machine with requirement ($v.r\_vCPU$, $v.r\_RAM$) to server s_{li} as virtual machine v_{k+1}. The constraints above have to be met also with the new VM, so we have the following constraints.

$$\sum_{j=1}^{k_{li}} v_j \cdot r\_vCPU * v_j \cdot a\_Urate + v_{k+1} \cdot r\_vCPU <=$$

$$<= k * s_{li} \cdot nr\_Core \tag{5}$$

$$\sum_{j=1}^{k_{li}} v_j \cdot a\_RAM + v_{k+1} \cdot r\_RAM <= s_{li} \cdot nr\_RAM \tag{6}$$

$$\sum_{j=1}^{k_{li}} v_j \cdot r\_vCPU + v_{k+1} \cdot r\_vCPU <=$$

$$<= s_{li} \cdot nr\_Core * \max vCPUpCore \tag{7}$$

$$k_{li} + 1 <= \max VMpServer \tag{8}$$

Before assigning the new VM to the server s_{li}, its energy consumption, E_{li0}, is

$$E_{li0} = f(U_{li0}) \tag{9}$$

and CPU usage rate is

$$U_{li0} = \frac{\sum_{j=1}^{k_{li}} v_j \cdot r\_vCPU * v_j \cdot a\_Urate}{s_{li} \cdot nr\_Core} \tag{10}$$

The total energy TE_{li0}, that data center used for the server s_{li} before assigning the new VM is

$$TE_{li0} = PUE_l * E_{li0} \tag{11}$$

The total CO_2 emission, C_{li0}, due to the server s_{li} in the data center before assigning the new VM is

$$C_{li0} = CUE_l * E_{li0} \tag{12}$$

After assigning, the energy consumption is

$$E_{li1} = f(U_{li1}) \tag{13}$$

where CPU usage rate is

$$U_{li1} = \frac{\sum_{j=1}^{k_{li}} v_j \cdot r\_vCPU * v_j \cdot a\_Urate + v_{k+1} \cdot r\_vCPU}{s_{li} \cdot nr\_Core} \tag{14}$$

If the goal is in optimizing energy, we have to pick the server s_{li} in a way that minimizes $(E_{li1}-E_{li0})$.

CO$_2$ emission is

$$C_{li1} = CUE_l * E_{li1} \tag{15}$$

If the goal is in optimizing CO$_2$ emission, we have to pick the sever s_{li} in a way that minimizes $(C_{li1}-C_{li0})$.

2.2   Global Optimization Request

When moving a virtual machine v_{li} from center d_l to center d_k, we have to consider the following constraints:

- Transfer time must be less than T
- Energy spent for the transfer must be less than E_t

After redistributing all running virtual machines over D, each server s_{li} has an updated set of running virtual machines V_{li1} including k_{li1} virtual machines. The new arrangement must also satisfy the above constraints (1)-(4).The total energy used in the federated data center is then

$$E_1 = \sum_{l=1}^{N} f(U_{li1}) \text{ with } i \in [1,n], l \in [1,N] \tag{16}$$

where n is the number of servers and N is the number of data centers, $f(U_{li1})$, and CPU usage rate is as follows

$$U_{li1} = \frac{\sum_{j=1}^{k_{i1}} v_j.r\_vCPU * v_j.a\_Urate}{s_{li}.nr\_Core} \tag{17}$$

CO$_2$ emission is

$$C_1 = \sum_{l=1}^{N} f(U_{li1}) * CUE_l \text{ with } i \in [1,n], j \in [1,N] \tag{18}$$

We have to rearrange the workload in a way that minimizes the CO$_2$ emission C_l.

If the goal is minimizing energy consumption, we also minimize C_l but with CUE_l replaced by PUE_l.

3   Algorithm for Single Allocation Request

The main idea of the proposed algorithm is to go through each server in each data center to see the consumed energy and CO_2 emission if we assign the VM to that server of the data center. From those collected data we will select the server of the data center having the smallest CO_2 emission. The algorithm for minimizing energy is similar.

The algorithm for single allocation request (see Fig. 1) is presented in Table 1. In order to satisfy the VM allocation request the algorithm tries to find a server with minimum energy overhead. To do so, the algorithm takes into consideration the information about data center (*data center description*), including the CUE, and considers the acting SLA. Besides, the algorithm communicates with the power calculator for the evaluation of required power resources. Based on all these parameters, the algorithm, finally, proposes the candidate server for the allocation.

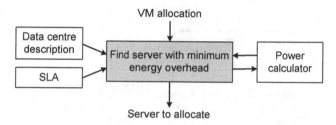

Fig. 1. Single allocation request diagram

The pseudo code provides the algorithm (see Table 1) explanation in more details and is as follows:

Table 1. Single allocation request for federated traditional data center

0	**Input**: model of all data centers in the federation, constraints,
1	characteristics of the incoming VM
2	Set b_meet=0
3	For each data center d_l
4	{
5	**Step 0**: The servers of d_l are in an array A_l
6	**Step 1**: Calculate power consumption P_l and CO_2
7	emission C_l of d_l
8	**Step 2**: Set i=0
9	**Step 3**: Check if the resources of the server
10	at array index i meet the requirement
11	**Step 4**: If not go to Step 8
12	**Step 5**: Calculate power consumption P_{li} and CO_2
13	emission C_{li} of the data center if the VM is
14	deployed on the server at array index i
15	**Step 6**: Save the tuple $(l, i, C_{li} - C_l)$
16	in a list L
17	**Step 7**: Set b_meet=1
18	**Step 8**: i++
19	**Step 9**: Repeat the process from Step 3 until i
20	exceeds the size of the array
21	}

Table 1. (*continued*)

22	If b_meet==1
23	Go through the list L to find the tuple having
24	the smallest C_{1i}- C_1
25	**Output**: the server in the data center having
26	the smallest C_{1i}- C_1
27	If b_meet==0
28	**Output**: no solution

4   Algorithm for Global Optimization Request

This section describes the algorithm for global optimization request (see Fig. 2).

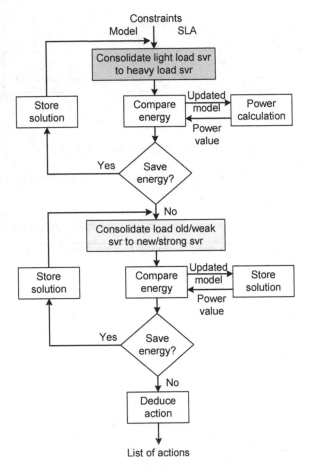

Fig. 2. Global optimization flow diagram

The main idea of the algorithm is to move all the heavy loading VMs to the servers which have the best rate of CO_2 emission or the largest computational horsepower. The VMs which cannot conveniently be moved out of the old data centers are rearranged inside the same data center to achieve the smallest possible CO_2 emission value. The same mechanism can be applied to optimize the energy by replacing CUE by PUE.

The algorithm for global allocation request for federated traditional data center is as follows:

Table 2. Global allocation request for federated traditional data center

0	**Input**: model of all data centers in the federation, constraints
1	**Step 0**: Form list of all VMs *LV* running in all data centers
2	**Step 1**: Form list of all servers *LS* in all data centers
3	**Step 2**: Sort the list *LV* in descending order of the actual CPU
4	usage *A*.
5	The actual CPU usage *A* of a VM *v* is calculated with
6	*A= v.r_vCPU * v.a_Urate*
7	**Step 3**: Sort the list *LS* in ascending order of the maximum CO_2
8	emission *E* per core of the server.
9	The maximum CO_2 emission *E* per core of the server *s* is calculated
10	with
11	*E= s.max_Power*CUE/s.nr_Core*
12	**Step 4**: For each server in the list *LS*, we use the traditional
13	pack algorithm to reassign VMs in the list *LV* to the server; then
14	remove reassigned VMs out of *LV*
15	**Step 5**: If there are still VMs in the list *LV*, we return the empty
16	exchange list
17	**Step 6**: From the new assignment, form the exchange list
18	**Output**: Exchange list containing VMs that should be moved to other
19	servers

Table 3. Pack algorithm for traditional data center

1	**Input**: The server, list of VMs *LV*, constraints about transfer time
2	
3	Algorithm:
4	**Step 1**: Determine the number of free resources in the server
5	(fCPU, fMem)
6	**Step 2**: (where nCPU and nMem is the number of CPU and size of RAM
7	available on the server, respectively):
8	For each VM in *LV*
9	{
10	if((fCPU*k < nCPU*u_rate) && (fMem < nMem))
11	{
12	Calculate the transfer time *TF* from old data
13	center to the one
14	If *TF* meets the transfer time constraints
15	Put VM into list L1
16	Update the amount of free resources:
17	fCPU -= nCPU*u_rate
18	fMem -= nMem
19	}
20	}
21	**Output**: L1

5   Simulation Results

This section presents the simulation scenario and results for the federated traditional data center case.

5.1   Simulation Scenario

The simulation is done to study the saving rate of the resource allocation mechanism in different resource configuration scenarios. To do the simulation, we use 4 server classes with single core, duel cores, quad cores and six cores. The main parameters for each server class are presented in Table 4.

Table 4. Server configuration

Server type (i)	Nr. CPU	Nr. Cores	P_{idle} CPU (W)	f_i (GHz)	RAM (MB)	Nr. Fan	Disk (MB)	P_{max} (W)
1	1	1	7.57	2.0	1000	4	400	102.22
2	1	2	9.88	2.0	2000	4	500	103.39
3	1	4	20.14	2.2	4000	5	800	171.70
4	1	6	22	2.4	6000	6	1000	229

We generated 3 resource configuration scenarios: modern data center, normal data center and old data center as in Table 5. In the normal data center the percentage of different server classes is fully balanced. In the old data center, the percentage of server classes with less cores is predominant.

Table 5. Resource scenarios

Scenario	Nr. Server type1	Nr. Server type2	Nr. Server type3	Nr. Server type4
Modern –1	50	100	150	200
Normal – 2	100	100	100	100
Old – 3	200	150	100	50

With each resource configuration, we generated a raw set of jobs. The jobs come randomly to the system within the period of 1000 time slots. The parameters for each job are determined by random selection. As the jobs in the traditional computing style scenario may have a long runtime period, we selected the runtime for each job spanning from 1 to 100 time slots. It should be noted that 1 time slot lasts 5 minutes.

We generated 3 federated data centers configurations: federated data centers with many old data centers, federated data centers with balanced types of data center, federated data centers with many modern data centers. The detail of each federated data centers configuration is presented in Table 6.

Table 6. Configuration of three federated data centers

Federated ID	Configuration	Nr. Old centers	Nr. Normal centers	Nr. Modern centers
1	Many Old	6	3	1
2	Balanced	3	4	3
3	Many Modern	1	3	6

We use 3 PUE/CUE configurations as presented in Table 7.

Table 7. PUE/CUE configurations

Type	Energy source	PUE	ESC	CUE
Low	Oil 20%, Hydro 40%, Nuclear 40%	1.3	0.12844	0.166792
Medium	Coal 50%, Nuclear 30%, Hydro 20%	1.5	0.45983	0.689745
High	Coal 80%, Oil 20%	1.8	0.85	1.53

To assign PUE/CUE to data center, we use 3 assigning configurations as presented in Table 8.

Table 8. Assigning configurations

Assign ID	Energy source
1	Old data center high PUE/CUE, normal data center normal PUE/CUE, modern data center low PUE/CUE
2	Old data center normal PUE/CUE, normal data center normal PUE/CUE, modern data center normal PUE/CUE
3	Old data center low PUE/CUE, normal data center normal PUE/CUE, modern data center high PUE/CUE

With each federated data centers configuration, with each PUE/CUE configuration, we run 3 simulation scenarios.

- Scenario 1: Each new VM will be allocated with the single allocation algorithm developed in phase 1 (see D4.1), in its own data center
- Scenario 2: Each new VM will be allocated with single federated allocation algorithm (see Chapter III.1.1.a.).
- Scenario 3: Each new VM will be allocated with single federated allocation algorithm (see Section 3). Every k timeslots, call global federated allocation algorithm.

For each scenario, calculate the Energy/CO_2 in 1000 timeslots where 1 timeslot is an arbitrary unit, which simulates 5 minutes of real time. We compare the result of the three aforementioned scenarios.

5.2   Results

The simulation results in terms of energy consumption (in MW*timeslot) are presented in Table 9.

Table 9. Simulation results for energy consumption

Feder ated ID	Assign ID	Single allocation - Energy	Single federated allocation Energy	Saving	Single + global federated allocation Energy	Transfer Energy	Saving
1	1	385.79	277.049	28%	265.6591	0.003442	31%
1	2	354.12	329.6796	7%	313.7542	0.003736	11%
1	3	338.59	289.3345	15%	275.3579	0.003646	19%
2	1	395.18	314.6082	20%	301.7559	0.049073	24%
2	2	396.13	369.2494	7%	354.1649	0.033214	11%
2	3	413.55	326.031	21%	312.712	0.004585	24%
3	1	412.09	357.4885	13%	343.6139	0.068402	17%
3	2	445.99	418.3728	6%	402.1352	0.003558	10%
3	3	502.17	367.9638	27%	353.6827	0.004252	30%

The energy saving rate achieved applying federated optimization compared to not applying it is also presented in Fig. 3.

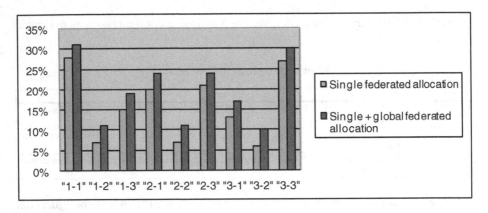

Fig. 3. Energy saving rate of applying federated optimization for traditional data centers

The simulation result in terms of CO_2 emission (in Ton*timeslot/h) is presented in Table 10.

Table 10. Simulation results for CO_2 emission.

Feder ated ID	Assig n ID	Single allocation - CO_2	Single federated allocation CO_2	Saving	Single + global federated allocation CO_2	Transfer CO_2	Saving
1	1	252.81	34.36192	86%	32.94925	0.00279	87%
1	2	162.83	151.5919	7%	144.2691	0.005537	11%
1	3	124.12	40.41604	67%	38.46371	0.008822	69%
2	1	183.24	37.32418	80%	35.79941	0.005822	80%
2	2	182.15	169.7897	7%	162.8534	0.003441	11%
2	3	233.33	45.11798	81%	43.27482	0.00734	81%
3	1	117.63	41.04069	65%	39.44785	0.007853	66%
3	2	205.08	192.3807	6%	184.9142	0.00496	10%
3	3	363.22	49.277	86%	47.3645	0.006843	87%

The CO_2 emission saving rate achieved applying federated optimization compared to not applying it is also presented in Fig.4.

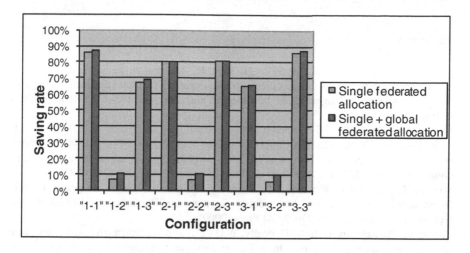

Fig. 4. CO_2 emission saving of applying federated optimization for traditional data centers

The simulation result shows the efficiency of the energy aware algorithms for the federated traditional data centers. Depending on the configuration, the saving rate spans from 10% to 31% in energy consumption and from 10% to 87% in CO_2 emission.

From the distribution of saving rate for both energy and CO_2 emission according to configurations, we can see that the federated optimization algorithm is very effective when the values of PUE/CUE of each data center in the federation is greatly differ from each other. Indeed, with the simulation configurations 1-2, 2-2 and 3-2, where the PUE/CUE values are the same for each data center, the saving rate is much smaller than in other configurations where the PUE/CUE values have a large variance.

6   Conclusions and Future Work

In this work we have proposed the optimization algorithms for resources management in a federated data center. To decrease the power consumption and carbon emission, we needed to find the servers with the lowest power consumption and shift the workload to these facilities. Simulations made with different types and configurations of data centers have shown that the power consumption saving can be up to 31% and carbon emission reduction can be up to 87%.

Our future work aims at applying the devised optimization algorithms in cloud data centers and evaluate the energy and carbon emission saving rates.

Acknowledgements. The authors would like to acknowledge the FIT4Green project (grant agreement no. 249020) sponsored by the European Commission. The authors also thank Mikko Majanen (VTT, Finland) for his valuable comments.

References

1. Dang, M.-Q., Basmadjian, R., De Meer, H., Lent, R., Mahmoodi, T., Sannelli, D., Mezza, F., Dupont, C.: Energy efficient resource allocation strategy for cloud data centres. In: 26th Int. Symposium on Computer and Information Sciences, pp. 133–141. Springer Press (2011)
2. Berl, A., Gelenbe, E., Di Girolamo, M., Giuliani, G., De Meer, H., Dang, M.-Q., Pentikousis, K.: Energy-Efficient Cloud Computing. J. Computer 53(7), 1045–1051 (2010)
3. Bradley, D.J., Harper, R.E., Hunter, S.W.: Workload-based power management for parallel computer systems. IBM J. of Research and Development 47(5-6), 703–718 (2003)
4. Meisner, D., Gold, B.T., Wenisch, T.F.: PowerNap: Eliminating server idle power. In: 14th International Conference on Architectural Support for Programming Languages and Operating Systems, pp. 205–216. ACM Press (2009)
5. Carrol, R., Balasubramaniam, S., Donnelly, W.D.: Dynamic optimization solution for green service migration in data centres. In: IEEE International Conference on Communications, pp. 1–6. IEEE Press (2011)
6. Barbagallo, D., Di Nitto, E., Dubois, D.J., Mirandola, R.: A Bio-inspired Algorithm for Energy Optimization in a Self-organizing Data Center. In: Weyns, D., Malek, S., de Lemos, R., Andersson, J. (eds.) SOAR 2009. LNCS, vol. 6090, pp. 127–151. Springer, Heidelberg (2010)
7. Berral, J.L., Goiri, I., Nou, R., Julia, F., Guitart, J., Gavalda, R., Torres, J.: Towards energy-aware scheduling in data centers using machine learning. In: 1st International Conference on Energy-Efficient Computing and Networking, pp. 215–224. ACM Press (2010)
8. Tang, Q., Gupta, S.K.S., Varsamopoulos, G.: Energy-efficient thermal-aware task scheduling for homogemeous high-performance computing data centers: a cyber-physical approach. IEEE Transactions on Parallel and Distributed Systems 19(11), 1458–1472 (2008)

DNA-Inspired Scheme for Building the Energy Profile of HPC Systems

Ghislain Landry Tsafack Chetsa[1,2], Laurent Lefevre[1], Jean-Marc Pierson[2], Patricia Stolf[2], and Georges Da Costa[2]

[1] INRIA, LIP Laboratory (UMR CNRS, ENS, INRIA, UCB)
Ecole Normale Superieure de Lyon, Université de Lyon, France
{ghislain.landry.tsafack.chetsa,laurent.lefevre}@ens-lyon.fr
[2] IRIT (UMR CNRS), University of Toulouse
118 Route de Narbonne, F-31062 Toulouse CEDEX 9, France
{stolf,dacosta,pierson}@irit.fr

Abstract. Energy usage is becoming a challenge for the design of next generation large scale distributed systems. This paper explores an innovative approach of profiling such systems. It proposes a DNA-like solution without making any assumptions on the running applications and used hardware. This profiling based on internal counters usage and energy monitoring allows to isolate specific phases during the execution and enables some energy consumption control and energy usage prediction. First experimental validations of the system modeling are presented and analyzed.

1 Introduction

Software solutions to improve the energy consumption of computing systems often fall into two categories, namely application-level solutions and system-level solutions. At the application level, a power-aware application design can use technologies such as Dynamic Voltage and Frequency Scaling (DVFS) for CPU energy reduction and the Low Power Idle (LPI) techniques for networks to reduce the application power usage at runtime with low performance penalty [12]. Code instrumentation can be used to adapt the processor's frequency and voltage according to the application's needs, so to reduce the application's overall power consumption [13,9,14]. Instrumented-code, inserted into the application source code, aims at dividing the application into regions having the same characteristics (memory intensive, CPU intensive, network intensive or disk intensive). The appropriate "power-saving" scheme (often the CPU frequency and voltage or P-state) is then selected for each defined region accordingly.

Software approaches could be very effective if a system designer (cloud or grid provider) has sufficient knowledge of the applications running on its system. For example an action applied to a single node may impact the power consumption of the remaining nodes running the same application and therefore the overall system energy consumption. Therefore, an effective use of these power saving

J. Huusko et al. (Eds.): E^{2}DC 2012, LNCS 7396, pp. 141–152, 2012.

schemes on a multi-node system require a view of the system as a whole. The commonly used approach consists of instrumenting the source program to determine when to trigger an action on a computing node and how to handle that action's side effects on the remaining nodes running the same application. Instrumenting the program source code requires a specific expertise from the platform provider, which can not be assumed. Our work overcomes that necessity of instrumenting the application source code in order to apply power saving schemes.

A large body of work highlights the effectiveness of high performance computing (HPC) applications' power and energy consumption estimation via dedicated system registers known as hardware monitoring counters or performance counters. Hardware monitoring counters provide a means to understanding an application's resource utilization patterns. Power or energy estimation models based on hardware performance counters are often tailored for a specific type of applications: Indeed a power consumption model built for a workload having frequent memory accesses may not fit well a workload having infrequent memory accesses, and the same goes for frequent disk/network accesses workloads. Hence we believe that it is necessary to model phases of applications instead of applications, and therefore it is first needed to recognize and identify the successive phases of the system.

This paper studies how to represent the system into different phases considering their power consumption and hardware performance counters (including disk read/write and network bytes received/sent count) accessed throughout the phase. Observations led us to the following assumptions: (a) Hardware performance counters are accurate predictors of the system's energy consumption, (b) Any change in the set of performance counters relevant to power consumption prediction over a given duration reflects a change in the system's computational state over that duration. Based on these assumptions, we propose an approach to model the whole system's runtime (from a single node system to a cluster system) as a sequence of phases where each phase exhibits a computational behavior. This modeling paves the way to providing fine-grained control of HPC application power consumption without a priori knowledge of the application.

The major contributions of this paper are the following:

- We propose a DNA-like system model in order to better control large scale systems energy consumption. We focus on dividing applications into different phases. Its effectiveness is proven experimentally.
- We develop a cross platform energy consumption prediction model as a use-case of our system modeling approach.

This paper is organized as follows. Background and related work are presented in Section 2. We propose a representation model denoted as "DNA-like" representation of a system in Section 3. Based on this model, we propose an application mapping to the system representation and present some experimental results in Section 4. Section 5 concludes and introduces future works.

2   Background

Many applications have recurring phases during execution. Many works investigate methods to use these phases for architectural and system adaptations. Weissel et al. propose to adapt processor execution by monitoring memory boundedness of applications [17] . Dhodapkar et al. investigate dynamic hardware reconfiguration [7]. Murali Annavaram and al. [1] also point out the use of sequential and parallel phases in parallel applications for efficient distribution of threads on an asymmetric multiprocessor. These works open the door to any kind of system's optimization based on phases recognition including controlling and limiting the power consumption of large-scale systems.

   A common approach to minimize the power consumption of large-scale systems is to identify phase-based applications [13]. The core idea is to schedule the processors to a higher frequency for CPU (Central Processing Unit) intensive phases, and to a lower frequency for non-CPU bound phases and workload [13,6]. Focusing on highly iterative applications which allow them to predict the future behavior of an application based on its past, Freeh et al. identify nodes having been assigned small computations to reduce their frequency [8]. These approaches are quite effective, however to our knowledge the source code of the application needs to be analyzed carefully to determine the different phases thus the CPU frequency at which each phase should run. Therefore, detecting phases is not only application specific but also requires extensive knowledge given the complexity of today's high performance applications. In comparison, our work does not attempt to estimate or reduce the system's power or energy consumption, instead, we investigate the possibility of detecting and characterizing application's execution phases at runtime for using insights gathered form hardware monitoring events and the system's energy consumption. The particularity of our approach is that it almost does not require any knowledge of the application under consideration.

3   DNA-Like System Modeling

As mentioned earlier in this paper, a fine-grained power control of a whole cluster system requires a view of that system as a whole. In this section, we introduce a very simple model for describing a system's runtime behavior. We assume a system or a cluster system is a set of computing nodes with their applicative states (the system state during application execution); network devices such as routers and switches are not taken into account. The strength of our model is that it provides insights about the system's computational state as well as its power/energy consumption. Our model represents a cluster system runtime as a state graph whose initial and final states are the system's idle state (or configuration). A transition from one state S1 to S2 is weighted by the conditional probability that the system goes to S2 given that it is in S1.

   We represent each system state including the idle state as a column vector of size n; where n is the number of computing nodes in the system, and whose entries describes the system behavior over a fixed period of time. An entry of a system's state vector is defined considering what we call the "DNA-like" structure of the system, which is a succession of computational behaviors exhibited by the system over time. We call such a computational behavior a "letter" and the set of possible computational behaviors the "system description alphabet".

A letter itself is modeled as a column vector of hardware monitoring counters including disk read/write and network bytes (respectively packets) sent/received counts to capture non memory- or CPU-intensive behavior. Details on their construction are provided later in this paper. On some platforms, it may not be possible to measure the system power/energy consumption using the power distribution unit. To avoid this limitation, one of our design constraint is that a letter in addition to describing the computational system, should provide a way to estimate the system power/energy consumption over a time period.

3.1   Letter Model

Observation. Efforts to model HPC applications power/energy consumption via performance monitoring counters have shown that performance monitoring counters relevant to power consumption estimation depend on the application itself. Thus performance counters relevant to power consumption estimation of a CPU intensive application may differ from those relevant to power consumption estimation of a memory intensive application.

As performance monitoring counters relevant to power consumption estimation depends on the computational state of the application, we state that *any change in the set of performance counters relevant to power consumption estimation of an application over a time period T reflects a change in the application computational state over the same time period T.*

Based on the above statement, we propose Algorithm 1 which takes as input an application footprint as a matrix and outputs the partition of the application into computational phases according to changes in the set of performance monitoring counters relevant to the power consumption estimation. Each row r of the input matrix contains values of hardware monitoring counters recorded over the sample interval timestamped r.

Relevant Hardware Counters Definition. The steps to find out which performance counters are relevant to power estimation are the following: (1) the most straightforward approach is to only take into account the first k performance counters highly correlated to power consumption, (2) the second approach relies on the power model described by $Power \sim \sum_{i=1}^{n} \alpha_i * C_i$ or a similar one (linear or not). In this equation α_i and C_i are model coefficients and hardware counters respectively. We conduct a multi-variable linear regression to obtain coefficients α_i and retain counters C_j exhibiting a 5% level of statistical significance to power consumption estimation given the power model.

Figures 1, where similar patterns refer to the same computational behavior, shows the output of our algorithm considering a constant number (4 in this case) of hardware counters. The system under consideration comprises two computing

---

Data: A: a matrix representing the application footprint, $P = \emptyset$
Result: P: a set containing subsets R_i representing application phases
Initialization: consider a sample interval S_n of upper bound n, n represents the
first n rows of the application matrix A such that $n > p + 1$, where p is the
number of performance counters (including disk read/write and network packets
(bytes) sent/received count).
$P = P \cup R_0$
while $row(A) > n$ **do**
$\quad$ Shift the upper bound of S to $n = upper\_bound(S) + n$
$\quad$ Compute the set R_i of relevant counters from S_n
$\quad$ **if** $R_{i-1} \neq R_i$ **then**
$\quad\quad$ Find $j \in [upper\_bound(S) - n, upper\_bound(S)]$ such that $R_j == R_{i-1}$,
$\quad\quad$ where R_j is the set of relevant counters from Sj;
$\quad\quad$ $P = P \cup R_j$
$\quad\quad$ Delete the first j rows of A
$\quad\quad$ Go to 1 (Initialization)
$\quad$ **end**
end

Algorithm 1. Algorithm to detect application phases

nodes running the NAS LU (class C problem on sixteen processes) benchmark [2]. The second approach showed bad results as the power estimation error using the power model is sometimes too high. We can also noticed that four phases was detected on the first computing node (on the x-axis from 0 to 60, form 60 to 90, from 90 to 120, and finally from 120 to 160) and five on the second computing node.

Letter Encoding and Representation. In this section, we present a formal representation of letters of our system description model. To simplify we consider that a letter has four hardware monitoring counters i.e., the number of hardware monitoring counters representing a letter is fixed to 4. We also limit the overall number of hardware monitoring counters to sixteen. Although it is possible to monitor more than 64 hardware counters on a single node of our cluster, only a few of them are relevant to the system's power consumption estimation [5,15].

Let's assign each hardware monitoring counter (including disk reads/writes and network (packets) sent/received bytes) to a four-bit aggregation or half byte. Our quadruplet is therefore of the form (X_1, X_2, X_3, X_4); where each X_i values is a half byte. Now, deleting commas in between the X_i gives a sixteen-bit aggregation which converted into decimal is an unsigned integer. The unsigned integer obtained from the above transformation is then the final representation of a letter.

3.2 System Model Use-Cases

This section proposes two simple use-cases of our system modeling approach. We first show how the system's energy profile can be derived from its model. Next,

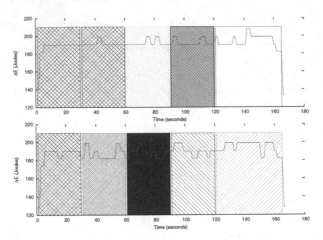

Fig. 1. Example of phase detection on a two-nodes cluster system running the NAS LU benchmark (from top to bottom, first and second computing node)

we present an approach to predict the energy consumption of an application using our system model and partial execution.

Energy Profiling. The concept of energy profile is very well defined in fields such as physical chemistry, but in computer science it is not easy to find an unanimous definition of this concept. The following definitions can be considered: For an application, the energy profile (respectively power profile) can be roughly defined as its energy (respectively power) footprint during its execution. This definition assumes that the application under consideration is the only application running on the system. A more complete definition presents an application's energy profile as its part of the energy footprint variation of the overall system during its execution.

In studies such as [5,11,4,16,3,10,18] efforts have been devoted to model power usage of system components (CPU, memory, disk, network) via hardware performance counters or hardware monitoring events. From those studies, the energy profile of an application can also be defined as a set of measurements (hardware monitoring events collected per-process or system-wide) over a time interval T such that there exists a combination of them estimating the power/energy used by the application or the whole system over T. The last definition describes the energy consumed by the application or the whole system via a set of hardware monitoring counters. This is particularly interesting as hardware monitoring counters in addition to providing insight about the system's (application's) computational state give way to compute its power consumption.

According to the hardware events-oriented definition of the energy profile, our system model implicitly defines its energy profile. For example, let's consider the energy profile in Figure 1 (a), which can be written as a sequence of the form $L_i \ldots X_i \ldots L_k$ denoted as its DNA-like structure; where each system phase is replaced by a letter L_i or XXX which refers to any system configuration or state we do not have enough information about (XXX may typically represent an idle state of the system). It is obvious that the system's energy profile is easy to obtain considering the application, for each known letter is associated to a specific power consumption.

Cross Platform Energy Consumption Prediction. This work is probably the very first attempt to predict energy consumption of an application on a given platform. The design of an energy prediction model is mainly motivated by the idea that users often have more than one candidate platforms for running their jobs, therefore choosing the less energy consuming platform can be beneficial to both users and platform providers.

Key concepts of our prediction model include *DNA-like structure of the application*, and *relative energy*. To simplify, we assume that the application under consideration is the only application running on the system, so the system's DNA-like structure is that of the application.

The model implicitly uses two sets of data, one from a reference platform provided by the DNA-like structure of the application, and one from a target platform which is the platform on which we want to estimate the overall energy consumption of the application. The aforementioned reference platform is the platform on which the pattern (DNA-like structure) matching with the application currently running was found.

As mentioned earlier, an application's run matches with a DNA-like structure if a significant percentage of the DNA-like structure matches with the already executed part of the application. Let E_{tar} be the energy consumed by the already executed part of the application and E_{ref} the energy that the matched part of the DNA-like structure had consumed on the reference platform. Denoted as E_{rel}, the relative energy consumption between the two platforms is given by the following: $E_{rel} = \frac{E_{tar}}{E_{ref}}$

With the above relative energy, the estimated energy consumption of the application is given by:

$$E_{est} = \int_0^{X\%} P(t)_{i,tar}\, dt + E_{rel} * \int_{X\%}^{end} P'(t)_{j,ref}\, dt$$

Where E_{est} is the estimated energy consumption on the target platform; E_{rel} the relative energy consumption between the target platform and the reference platform. In the above equation, $\int_0^{X\%} P(t)_{i,tar}\, dt$ represents the energy consumed by the application before a match is found with a pattern from the profile database. Either measured or estimated, $P(t)_{i,tar}$ is the instantaneous power usage of the application. $P'(t)_{j,ref}$ is the instantaneous power usage of the application on the reference platform and can be obtained from its DNA-like structure.

We define the estimation accuracy as the ratio between the estimated and measured energy on the target platform.

4 Experimental Results: Model Development and Validation

We design a cluster composed of 2 nodes with 2 Intel Quad-core Xeon CPUs each (16 cores in total), 12 GB of RAM. The nodes are connected by a Gigabit Ethernet switch. The Linux kernel 3.1.1 is installed on each node where perf event is used to read the hardware monitoring counters. MPICH is used as MPI library. MG, LU, IS, CG, EP, SP, and BT from NPB-3.3 are used for the experiments. MG demonstrates the capabilities of a very simple multi-grid solver, MG nodes communicate with their neighbors, and with other "distant" nodes. IS calculates the large-scale integer sorting. The CG kernel communication graph involves lots of neighbor communication. EP is embarrassingly parallel code that implements the random-number generator. Each application has several types of computations, memory access, and communication phases. Class C of these benchmarks are used (they are compiled using the default compiler's options). Each node's power usage is monitored with one sample per second using a power distribution unit.

4.1 Idle System State

We conduct experiments to observe the degree to which diverse hardware events affect the system's idle power consumption. Results show that they are almost never the same from a time interval T to another and that the system's idle power cannot be correlated with hardware events. Hence, to characterize the system's idle state, we monitor it again under different workload characteristics. The number of cache misses are chosen as the main system characteristic.

As shown in Figure 2, the number of cache misses normalized to the elapsed cycles count (yielding the event rate) clearly discriminates among all workloads (each scatter of points represents one NAS banchmark). Based on this observation, we define a threshold β under which the system is said to be idle. We assign the letter XXX to the system's idle state to reflect the fact that we are unable to estimate its power usage via hardware performance counters.

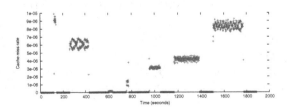

Fig. 2. NAS benchmarks characterized by their cache miss rate

4.2   Computational States

Firstly, we execute each of the above listed benchmarks 30 times and record the number of occurrences of each performance counter in Table 1. These performance counters are recorded every second along with the power consumption of each node of our cluster. Next, we run Algorithm 1 for defining regions for each node in order to create the system description alphabet. Once the alphabet of each node computed, we use the run history to create a transition matrix for each node. The transition matrix typically gives the probability to move from one letter to another.

As evaluation, we first investigate how close to reality is our approach for partitioning an application into different computational behaviors (or simply phases). For this purpose, we run successively two applications opposite from their computational point (i.e. IS and EP). IS is communication intensive whereas EP is mainly computing. Figure 3 shows the effectiveness of our approach. The couple of integers appearing in each region of the figure gives for each region the corresponding letter coded as an unsigned integer and its duration. For example, (17692 21) means the hardware events highlighted in bold in Table 1 are relevant to power consumption estimation over 21 seconds for the second computing node. We observe from the experiments that two phases were detected and identified with different letters for the two nodes nodes, and that their energy consumptions are different.

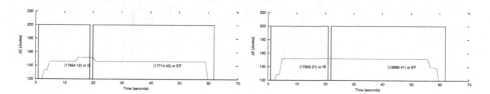

Fig. 3. Dividing NAS benchmarks IS and EP ran successively into two different computational behaviors using their power usage and hardware counters (left: First node; right: Second node)

Table 1. List of hardware monitoring counters

PERF_COUNT_HW_CPU_CYCLES	PERF_COUNT_HW_INSTRUCTIONS
PERF_COUNT_HW_CACHE_REFERENCES	PERF_COUNT_HW_STALLED_CYCLES_FRONTEND
PERF_COUNT_HW_CACHE_MISSES	PERF_COUNT_HW_BUS_CYCLES
PERF_COUNT_HW_BRANCH_INSTRUCTIONS	PERF_COUNT_HW_BRANCH_MISSES
netSENTbyte	netSENTpkt
netRECVbyte	netRECVpkt
Write I/O	Read I/O

Use Case Evaluation: Energy Profile. The goal of our approach is to use the energy profile to predict the energy consumption and optimize the resources used. So, if we are able to predict the next system configuration, it will no longer be necessary to instrument the application source code prior to applying power saving schemes. For example if the predictor tells that the next state is a communication phase with an acceptable error, then power-saving schemes such as DVFS could be triggered. To observe to what degree our system model fits that expectation, we follow this generic methodology:

- Run the application and create its alphabet using Algorithm 1. We assume that all letters have the same duration of fifteen seconds, i.e., each letter covers fifteen seconds of the application's lifetime.
- Take the first two letters of the same application and attempt to determine the rest of the sequence using the system transition matrix.

We discuss the results for LU because it runs a long time. The DNA-like structure (or description sequence) for one node running LU benchmark is provided in Figure 4, where durations are omitted (all 15s). We apply our predictor to the second letter of the LU sequence (293,15) to determine its energy profile or the rest of the sequence (recall that an application's energy profile is derived from its DNA-like structure or description sequence). The predictor simply looks at the transition matrix and chooses the next state with the highest probability. Using this approach, we are only able to predict a few parts of the entire application – less than 5 letters in this case. This can be attributed to the simplicity of the predictor. We are currently investigating more complex approaches to enhance our prediction mechanism.

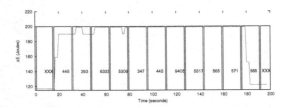

Fig. 4. DNA-like representation with fixed letter duration for a node running the LU benchmark

Evaluation for Energy Consumption Prediction. We evaluate our model for energy consumption prediction considering a very stable application. For simplicity, we only predict the energy consumption of one node. The application iteratively does two things: It first computes the inverse of a 10x10 square matrix and then it copies a large file from a remote host. We choose such an application to ensure that its behavior is stable enough over time. The advantage of having a stable application resides in the fact that we can successfully predict the entire execution of the application.

We consider two scenarios. For the first scenario, the target and reference platforms are the same node but running at respectively 1.6GHz and 2.13GHz. For the second scenario, the reference platform is a Dell Power Edge server and the target platform a Sun Fire V20z. For partial execution, 20% of the application is executed. Results are summarized in Table 2. We compute for both scenarios the expected energy consumption based on the equations given in Section 3.2. We can see from those results that the accuracy is very good. Notice that the accuracy is higher because it is computed considering the average energy consumption instead of the peak energy consumption. However it must be noted that the considered application is very simple and stable.

Table 2. Energy consumption prediction results summary

Scenario	Estimated Energy (in Joules)	Accuracy	Peak energy consumption
1	797143.5	1.01	811932
2	2068515.6	1.02	2088515.6

5 Conclusions and Future Work

In this paper we propose to optimize large-scale systems energy consumption by triggering specific actions to reduce energy consumption depending on the behavior of the application being executed. We introduce a system modeling approach and some use cases. as a state graph and present some relevant use cases of the model. Our approach for dividing applications into phases is fast and does not require extensive knowledge of applications running on the system. We show through experiments that our model can effectively be used for predicting the system's energy profile. We also show that energy consumption estimation using our system model and partial execution can successfully predict the entire system power usage.

Future work will combine our model with power saving schemes. We will also improve the system model using more sophisticated mechanisms in order to guarantee accurate energy profile prediction. We also plan on using our energy consumption prediction model for predicting the energy consumption of real workloads on multi-nodes systems

Acknowledgments. This work is supported by the INRIA large scale initiative Hemera focused on "developing large scale parallel and distributed experiments".

References

1. Annavaram, M., Grochowski, E., Shen, J.P.: Mitigating amdahl's law through epi throttling. In: ISCA, pp. 298–309. IEEE Computer Society (2005)
2. Bailey, D.H., Barszcz, E., Barton, J.T., Carter, R.L., Lasinski, T.A., Browning, D.S., Dagum, L., Fatoohi, R.A., Frederickson, P.O., Schreiber, R.S.: The nas parallel benchmarks. International Journal of High Performance Computing Applications 5, 63–73 (1991)
3. Bautista, D., Sahuquillo, J., Hassan, H., Petit, S., Duato, J.: A simple power-aware scheduling for multicore systems when running real-time applications. In: IPDPS, pp. 1–7. IEEE (2008)
4. Contreras, G.: Power prediction for intel xscale processors using performance monitoring unit events. In: Proceedings of the International Symposium on Low Power Electronics and Design (ISLPED), pp. 221–226. ACM Press (2005)

5. Costa, G.D., Hlavacs, H.: Methodology of measurement for energy consumption of applications. In: GRID, pp. 290–297. IEEE (2010)
6. Curtis-Maury, M., Dzierwa, J., Antonopoulos, C.D., Nikolopoulos, D.S.: Online power-performance adaptation of multithreaded programs using hardware event-based prediction. In: Egan, G.K., Muraoka, Y. (eds.) ICS, pp. 157–166. ACM (2006)
7. Dhodapkar, A.S., Smith, J.E.: Managing multi-configurable hardware via dynamic working set analysis. In: 29th Annual International Symposium on Computer Architecture, pp. 233–244 (2002)
8. Freeh, V.W., Kappiah, N., Lowenthal, D.K., Bletsch, T.K.: Just-in-time dynamic voltage scaling: Exploiting inter-node slack to save energy in mpi programs. J. Parallel Distrib. Comput. 68(9), 1175–1185 (2008)
9. Ge, R., Feng, X., Cameron, K.W.: Performance-constrained distributed dvs scheduling for scientific applications on power-aware clusters. In: Proceedings of the 2005 ACM/IEEE conference on Supercomputing, SC 2005, p. 34. IEEE Computer Society, Washington, DC (2005)
10. Joseph, R., Martonosi, M.: Run-time power estimation in high performance microprocessors. In: International Symposium on Low Power Electronics and Design, pp. 135–140 (2001)
11. Kadayif, I., Chinoda, T., Kandemir, M., Vijaykirsnan, N., Irwin, M.J., Sivasubramaniam, A.: vec: virtual energy counters. In: Proceedings of the 2001 ACM SIGPLAN-SIGSOFT Workshop on Program Analysis for Software Tools and Engineering, PASTE 2001, pp. 28–31. ACM, New York (2001)
12. Kansal, A., Zhao, F.: Fine-grained energy profiling for power-aware application design. SIGMETRICS Perform. Eval. Rev. 36, 26–31 (2008)
13. Kimura, H., Imada, T., Sato, M.: Runtime energy adaptation with low-impact instrumented code in a power-scalable cluster system. In: Proceedings of the 2010 10th IEEE/ACM International Conference on Cluster, Cloud and Grid Computing, CCGRID 2010, pp. 378–387. IEEE Computer Society, Washington, DC (2010)
14. Lim, M.Y., Freeh, V.W., Lowenthal, D.K.: Adaptive, transparent frequency and voltage scaling of communication phases in mpi programs. In: Proceedings of the 2006 ACM/IEEE Conference on Supercomputing, SC 2006. ACM, New York (2006)
15. Lively, C., Wu, X., Taylor, V., Moore, S., Chang, H.-C., Su, C.-Y., Cameron, K.: Power-aware predictive models of hybrid (MPI/OpenMP) scientific applications on multicore systems. In: Computer Science - Research and Development, pp. 1–9 (August 2011)
16. Singh, K., Bhadauria, M., McKee, S.A.: Real time power estimation and thread scheduling via performance counters. SIGARCH Comput. Archit. News 37, 46–55 (2009)
17. Weissel, A., Bellosa, F.: Process cruise control-event-driven clock scaling for dynamic power management. In: Proceedings of the International Conference on Compilers, Architecture and Synthesis for Embedded Systems (CASES 2002), Grenoble, France (2002)
18. Wu, W., Jin, L., Yang, J., Liu, P., Tan, S.X.D.: A systematic method for functional unit power estimation in microprocessors. In: Design Automation Conference (2006)

Author Index